Financial Management
in the Digital Economy

Singapore University of Social Sciences - World Scientific Future Economy Series

ISSN: 2661-3905

Series Editor
David Lee Kuo Chuen *(Singapore University of Social Sciences, Singapore)*

Subject Editors
Guan Chong *(Singapore University of Social Sciences, Singapore)*
Ding Ding *(Singapore University of Social Sciences, Singapore)*

Singapore University of Social Sciences - World Scientific Future Economy Series introduces the new technology trends and challenges that businesses today face, financial management in the digital economy, blockchain technology, smart contract and cryptography. The authors describe current issues that the business leaders and finance professionals are facing, as well as developments in digitalisation. The series covers several increasingly important new areas such as the fourth industrial revolution, Internet of Things (IoT), blockchain technology, artificial intelligence (AI) and many other forces of disruption and breakthroughs that shape today's realities of the economy. A better understanding of the changing environment in the future economy can enable business professionals and leaders to recognise realities, embrace changes, and create new opportunities — locally and globally — in this inevitable digital age.

Published*

Vol. 6   *Financial Management in the Digital Economy*
         edited by David Lee Kuo Chuen, Ding Ding and Guan Chong

Vol. 5   *The Digital Transformation of Property in Greater China: Finance, 5G, AI, and Blockchain*
         by Paul Schulte, Dean Sun and Roman Shemakov

Vol. 4   *Blockchain and Smart Contracts: Design Thinking and Programming for FinTech*
         by Lo Swee Won, Wang Yu and David Lee Kuo Chuen

Vol. 3   *Artificial Intelligence, Data and Blockchain in a Digital Economy, First Edition*
         edited by David Lee Kuo Chuen, supported by Singapore University of Social Sciences and World Scientific, in support of Singapore Digital (SG:D) and in collaboration with Infocomm Media Development Authority

*More information on this series can also be found at
https://www.worldscientific.com/series/susswsfes

(Continued at end of book)

Singapore University of Social Sciences - World Scientific
Future Economy Series : 6

Financial Management in the Digital Economy

Editors

David LEE Kuo Chuen
DING Ding
GUAN Chong

Singapore University of Social Sciences, Singapore

SUSS
SINGAPORE UNIVERSITY
OF SOCIAL SCIENCES

World Scientific

Published by

World Scientific Publishing Co. Pte. Ltd.

5 Toh Tuck Link, Singapore 596224

USA office: 27 Warren Street, Suite 401-402, Hackensack, NJ 07601

UK office: 57 Shelton Street, Covent Garden, London WC2H 9HE

Library of Congress Cataloging-in-Publication Data
Names: Lee, David (David Kuo Chuen), editor. | Ding, Ding, 1979–   editor. | Guan, Chong, editor.
Title: Financial management in the digital economy / editors, David Kuo Chuen Lee, Ding Ding,
    Chong Guan, Singapore University of Social Sciences, Singapore.
Description: Hackensack, NJ : World Scientific, 2022. | Series: Singapore university of
    social sciences - world scientific future economy series, 2661-3905 ; Vol. 6 |
    Includes bibliographical references and index.
Identifiers: LCCN 2021040777 | ISBN 9789811230004 (hardcover) |
    ISBN 9789811231452 (paperback) | ISBN 9789811230011 (ebook) |
    ISBN 9789811230028 (ebook other)
Subjects: LCSH: Financial services industry--Technological innovations. | Banks and banking--
    Data processing. | Blockchains (Databases) | Cryptocurrencies.
Classification: LCC HG1709 .L44 2022 | DDC 332.10285--dc23/eng/20211013
LC record available at https://lccn.loc.gov/2021040777

British Library Cataloguing-in-Publication Data
A catalogue record for this book is available from the British Library.

For any available supplementary material, please visit
https://www.worldscientific.com/worldscibooks/10.1142/12092#t=suppl

Desk Editors: Balasubramanian Shanmugam/Yulin Jiang

Typeset by Stallion Press
Email: enquiries@stallionpress.com

About the Editors

Dr David LEE Kuo Chuen is a Professor at the Singapore University of Social Sciences (SUSS) and Vice President of the Economic Society of Singapore. He is the founder of several entities, including BlockAsset Ventures; the external advisor to Stanford University's Distributed Trust Initiative; a Fulbright Scholar; and an Independent Director of listed and technology companies. He graduated with BSc, MSc, and PhD degrees in Econometrics from the London School of Economics and Political Science. He was the Director of the Sim Kee Boon Institute for Financial Economics and the Group Managing Director of OUE and Auric Pacific. He founded the Ferrell hedge fund in 1998 and was a property developer. He has more than 60 cited articles and 9 books on Asian economics, digital currency, blockchain, and inclusive FinTech. His latest book is entitled *Blockchain and Smart Contracts: Design Thinking and Programming for FinTech*.

Dr DING Ding is an Associate Professor and the Vice Dean of School Business at Singapore University of Social Sciences (SUSS), where she has worked since 2008. She holds a PhD in Economics and is a Chartered Financial Analyst (CFA). In her academic career, she has taught various economics and finance courses at the undergraduate, post-graduate, and executive training levels. Her recent research focuses on the development and application of FinTech, and she has published several books and articles in this field. She has also conducted workshops and seminars in the area of

FinTech and Blockchain and has developed courses to help students understand and adapt to the new digital economy.

Dr GUAN Chong is an Associate Professor in Marketing and Deputy Director in the Office of Graduate Studies, Singapore University of Social Sciences (SUSS), Singapore. Chong completed her PhD in Marketing at Nanyang Business School, Nanyang Technological University, and her undergraduate studies in Marketing at Guanghua School of Management, Peking University, China. Her research interests lie in the area of consumer decision-making on digital platforms. Her publications appear in leading journals such as *European Journal of Marketing, Journal of Interactive Marketing, Journal of Business Research, Telecommunications Policy, Psychology & Marketing*, and *DATABASE*. She is an editorial board member of *Internet Research*. Chong has taught various digital marketing courses at the undergraduate, graduate, and executive levels. She has consulted business practices and conducted corporate trainings on social media analytics, AI in marketing, and other emerging areas.

About the Authors

Dr TAN Chong Hui is an Associate Professor and the Head of the Finance Programme at the School of Business at the Singapore University of Social Sciences (SUSS), where he has been a faculty member since 2013. He graduated from UCLA with a PhD in Mathematics. He has rich experience in teaching computational and quantitative finance as well as applied computing technology to undergraduate and post-graduate students. He has also conducted executive training programmes in the finance industry. His research interest lies in the areas of FinTech, human sociality, and semantic modeling.

Dr Calvin M. L. CHAN is an Associate Professor and Director (Office of Graduate Studies) at the Singapore University of Social Sciences (SUSS). He received his PhD from the National University of Singapore and BSc(Hon) from the University of Warwick. His research focuses on the digital transformation of the public sector (e.g. e-government initiatives), the private sector (especially small and medium enterprises), and also the people sector (especially in the area of digitalization and aging). His research has been published in the *Information Systems Journal, European Journal of Information Systems, Journal of Strategic Information Systems, Journal of the American Society for Information Science and Technology* and the *Government Information Quarterly*. He has served on government committees pertaining to digitalization and aging, as Track Chair of conferences such as *Pacific Asia Conference on Information Systems* and *IRMA Conference*, and is on the Editorial Board of the *Pacific Asia Journal of the Association for Information Systems*.

Dr YU Yinghui is an Associate Professor who heads the Master of Finance programme and the Graduate Diploma in Financial Technology programme at the Singapore University of Social Sciences (SUSS). She obtained her PhD in Finance from University of Hong Kong in 2006, and before joining SUSS she was a derivatives trader with a global investment bank for eight years. Her research interests include asset pricing, alternative investments, risk management, as well as financial technologies and innovations. Her research has been published in journals such as the *Journal of Finance*.

Dr LIU Wenting is Senior Lecturer in Business Analytics Programme, Singapore University of Social Sciences (SUSS), Singapore. Wenting completed her PhD in Industrial Systems Engineering and Management at National University of Singapore. Her research interests lie in machine learning and statistical analysis, business forecasting, optimization model, and knowledge management.

Dr LAU Jing Feng graduated with a PhD in Mathematics from Purdue University. He has held research fellow positions at Tel Aviv University and National University of Singapore. In 2016, he joined Singapore University of Social Sciences (SUSS), where he has been appointed as the Head of the Mathematics Programme.

Dr HUNG Yu-chen is a Senior Lecturer of Marketing at the Singapore University of Social Sciences (SUSS). Her teaching expertise is in digital platform strategy, integrated marketing communication, business-to-business marketing, consumer behavior, and global marketing. Her research interests include innovation adoption, consumer psychology, and experiential marketing. Her works have appeared in various international journals, such as *International Journal of Research in Marketing*, *European Journal of Marketing*, *Journal of Business Research*, and *Journal of Marketing Management*.

Mr CHOO Teck Li studied in the pioneer batch of Master of Finance and Graduate Diploma (Fintech) at Singapore University of Social Sciences (SUSS), focusing on frontier technologies such as blockchain, AI, and cloud. He has spent years in a reputable investment company headquartered in Singapore, focusing on PE/VC in Asia. He has also invested venture to growth stage fund and directed deals across North Asia, SE Asia, US, and Europe. He is well-acquainted with middle office operations and systems, and is a project committee member for office digital transformation.

Mr TAY Kok Choon is a doctoral candidate with the Singapore University of Social Sciences. He is currently pursuing his research on how leadership orchestrates digital transformation. As a human resource professional, he is passionate about helping others to build better life with better careers. He has rich industry experience, covering areas such as business development, marketing as well as merger and acquisition.

Contents

Chapter 1

Bitcoin Blockchain Explained: Development and Challenges

Yu Yinghui and Tan Chong Hui

1.1 The Bitcoin Landscape

Bitcoin surfaced in November 2008 when Satoshi Nakamoto posted an article titled *Bitcoin: A Peer-to-Peer Electronic Cash System* on the Internet (Nakamoto, 2008). In January 2009, the bitcoin network was born with the issuance of the first bitcoins. Twelve years later, in 2021, there were over 70 million bitcoin wallet users and the price of 1 bitcoin was about US$39,000.

Over the years since its inception, Bitcoin has inspired other cryptocurrencies. Over 700 cryptocurrencies have arisen and a dozen has a market capitalization above $10 million each. One of the most notable among these is the *Ether*. The inventor of the Ether, Vitalik Buterin, has in fact created an entire computational platform, called the Ethereum, to handle smart contracts. His idea is that what the underlying technology is enabling is not merely currencies, but contracts that reside on the Internet which use cryptographic techniques to enforce trust and consensus that are normally associated with them.

Roughly speaking, a cryptocurrency is a peer-to-peer network accounting system that keeps track of who possesses how much of the currency. This is done by recording all transactions involving the transfer of currency from one peer to another in a data storage facility called the blockchain. The blockchain remembers the entire history of the network from its inception and thus enforces the integrity of the system.

Blockchain is currently spurring the development of the FinTech industry. It is reported that DTCC, a US post-trade services group that processes more than US$1,500 trillion of securities a year, will use technology from IBM and US blockchain start-ups R3 and Axoni as the basis for its next-generation trade information warehouse (Murphy, 2017). TP ICAP, one of the world's largest inter-dealer broker, announced that it is set to launch a cryptoasset trading platform for institutional investors in collaboration with Fidelity and others (TP ICAP, 2021).

1.1.1 *Peer-to-Peer Networks on the Internet*

A peer-to-peer (P2P) network is a network of communicating nodes that is decentralized. A node corresponds to a software that is downloaded from the web — this is called the client. Each client stores the necessary rules and methods for it to join the network and to communicate with other nodes. As the nodes interact, the state of the system is captured by the nodes. No single node has the entire picture of the system. The entire picture is broken down into bits and stored throughout the nodes.

The first globally successful P2P network is the BitTorrent. The protocol — i.e., the rules by which the nodes communicate — was designed by Bram Cohen in 2001. At one time, it was said to be responsible for 50% of Internet traffic and 75% of P2P traffic. In the BitTorrent protocol, nodes are either peers, leechers, or trackers. A peer is one instance of a BitTorrent client running on a computer on the Internet to which other clients connect and transfer data. A leecher is a downloader of data or a node that has a negative impact to the network. A tracker keeps track of the nodes and the data that is flowing around. A file, such as video, is broken down into parts, called seeds, which are sent to the various peers in the network, to be finally reassembled for the downloader.

P2P networks underlie some financial networks on the Internet, notably cryptocurrencies. For example, the lending network Prosper[1] is also P2P in nature. Appreciating how they function and their characteristics is important to the understanding of cryptocurrencies in general and blockchain-based systems like Ethereum.

1.1.2 *Open-Source Software Communities*

Internet software is not created out of thin air. There are communities of motivated and intelligent individuals who contribute to them. These communities are not disorganized or anarchic. The social structure evolves around a core of contributors and is very often centered around an individual who contributed the core code that got the project started in the first place. Outside the core is a community of volunteers who contribute in various ways to the project, generally with lower levels of consistency or intensity as compared to the core group.

It is important to appropriately situate the developer community and its core in the overall scheme of things. For instance, in a cryptocurrency open-source project, the initial contributors tend to gain a great deal if the value of the currency appreciates relative to the dollar as the project gains traction as they own significant amounts of the currency when it was still relatively without value at initial stages. Another illustration is the infamous DAO[2] hack incident, where Ethereum developers were forced to fork the project (Wong and Kar, 2016). This was a major decision in the life of the Ethereum project. While the decision is arrived at through the community, the actual decision-making process had to be negotiated through a definite social structure. Thus, though the software underlying P2P clients are open source and the network is touted

---

[1]https://www.prosper.com/
[2]The DAO (abbreviation for Decentralized Autonomous Organization) was a form of investor-directed venture capital fund on the Ethereum blockchain, whose objective was to provide a decentralized autonomous model where rules were set and executed through code.

to be decentralized, the developer core has a significant clout in the ecosystem.

1.2 Emergence of the Original Blockchain

1.2.1 *Definition*

Bitcoin can refer to either the protocol or the network.

The Bitcoin protocol is the structure, akin to a Lego blocks structure, that was put together by Satoshi Nakamoto, behind the implementation of the Bitcoin network. The key components are:

- P2P network
- Proof-of-Work consensus mechanism to achieve Byzantine fault tolerance
- Blockchain
- Cryptocurrency

The Bitcoin network is the P2P network that has arisen based on the Bitcoin protocol. The growth of the network is via an organic process: anyone can join and leave the system on his own free will.

The term "bitcoin," spelt with a lowercase b, refers to the cryptocurrency that arises from within the system.

1.2.2 *Chronology of Events*

The following lists key events in the historical evolution of the Bitcoin protocol and network, together with a smattering of events that indicate the extent of the ecosystem that emerges from and around the network:

- November 2008: Satoshi Nakamoto publishes the White Paper titled "Bitcoin: A Peer-to-Peer Electronic Cash System," outlining the idea behind a P2P-based cryptocurrency system
- January 2009: The first open source Bitcoin client was released and the Bitcoin network came into existence, with issuance of first bitcoins
  - One of the earliest exchanges between bitcoins and things outside the Bitcoin network: 2 Papa John's pizzas were purchased with 10,000 bitcoins

○ Satoshi Nakamoto assigned the lead developer status to Gavin Andresen and disappeared

○ First and hitherto (relative to 2017) only security vulnerability opened up and exploited: a transaction was created to produce 184 billion bitcoins and sent to 2 addresses; this was discovered on the same day, erased from the blockchain, and the bug was rectified

○ Mt. Gox started operating as bitcoin exchange

- 2011: Other cryptocurrencies started to emerge
- June 2012: Coinbase founded
- March 2013: First major fork in the Bitcoin blockchain

○ A bitcoin miner running version 0.8.0 of the bitcoin software created a large block that was considered invalid in version 0.7 due to an undiscovered inconsistency between the two versions, which has since been fixed

- November 2013: BTCUSD crossed and peaked at slightly over US$ 1,000
- December 2013: Li Ka-shing invested in BitPay, a bitcoin payment service provider based in Atlanta, Georgia, USA
- February 2014: Mt. Gox collapsed
- April 2014: Gavin Andresen stepped down as lead developer
- December 2015–January 2016: Segregated Witness (SegWit) vs Bitcoin Unlimited

○ Bitcoin protocol's capacity capacity was being tested
  For Bitcoin protocol, it takes about 10 minutes to process one block, which roughly equals 1 megabyte and contains about 2,000 transactions

○ Two camps arose from Bitcoin users: Core vs Unlimited
  Bitcoin Core wanted to keep the block size while reducing transaction size by a method known as SegWit; the change would be effectuated by a soft fork. Bitcoin Unlimited endorsed larger blocks; the change would be effectuated by a hard fork

- April 2016: Russia planned law to jail users of cryptocurrencies
- July 20, 2016: Hard fork occurred on Ethereum, splitting it into Ethereum and Ethereum Classic

- April 2017: Japan passed a law to accept bitcoin as a legal payment method
- April 2017: Russia signalled legitimizing Bitcoin in 2018
- May 2017: Bitcoin price neared US$2,500 for the first time in history
- August 1, 2017: The hard fork which enabled increased block size took place and Bitcoin Cash was created as a spinoff. Bitcoin Cash used 8-megabyte blocks instead of the 1-megabyte blocks used by the original Bitcoin, making it easier to scale as more people interact with the service
- October 2017: Another hard fork took place and Bitcoin Gold was generated, with the goal of making bitcoin mining a more equitable process that only required basic equipment for mining. It is mined on standard graphics processing units instead of the specific and more expensive hardware (ASICs) used exclusively for bitcoin mining.
- December 10, 2017: The Chicago Board Options Exchange started trading bitcoin futures
- December 17, 2017: The Chicago Mercantile Exchange started trading bitcoin futures
- January–March 2018: Bitcoin price fell from a high of nearly US$20,000 down to below US$8,000, and stayed below or around US$10,000 until the end of 2019
- March 2019: Medium.com published an article "Plan B" (2019), which attempted to describe the historic evolution of the Bitcoin price using the Stock-to-Flow macroeconomic model
- December 2020: Bitcoin price went back up to historic high of US$20,000 and continued higher all the way to US$58,332 on February 22, 2021 (Figure 1.1).

1.2.3   *The Key Components of the Bitcoin Protocol*

The Bitcoin protocol implements cryptocurrencies as a chain of transactions. The transactions are conducted within a P2P network, without the existence of a trusted central party.

The authenticity of the transactions must therefore be realized differently. This is done by publicly announcing each transaction

Bitcoin Price in USD

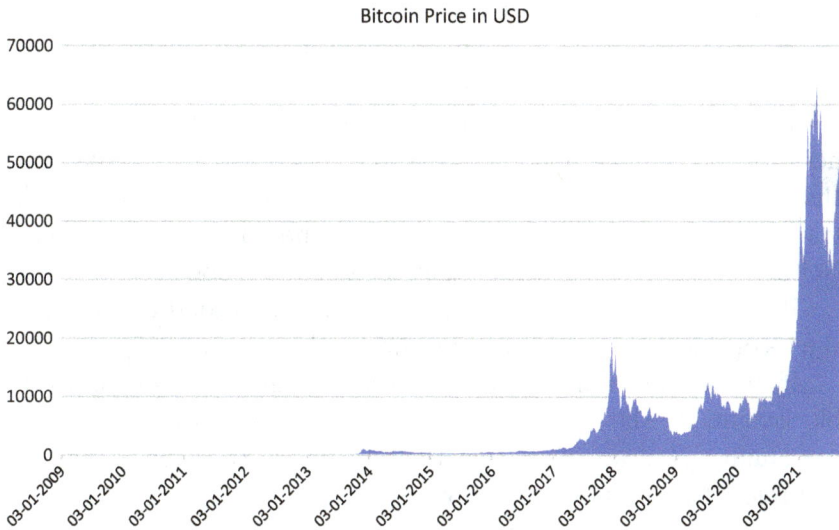

Figure 1.1: Bitcoin price skyrocketed in early 2021.

to the whole network. Once it becomes common knowledge that is accepted by everyone in the network, it becomes a fact.

This is the procedure in more detail:

(1) New transactions are broadcast to all nodes.
(2) Each node collects new transactions into a block.
(3) Each node works on finding a difficult Proof-of-Work for its block.
(4) When a node finds a Proof-of-Work, it broadcasts the block to all nodes.
(5) Nodes accept the block only if all transactions in it are valid and not already spent.
(6) Nodes express their acceptance of the block by working on creating the next block in the chain, using the hash of the accepted block as the previous hash.

Once a transaction goes into a block, and the block goes in the blockchain, it is accepted by everyone in the system to be a fact. This is coded into the protocol.

Suppose there are two transactions that are broadcasted at the same time from a node, each spending the same bitcoins. This is the so-called double-spend problem.

These two transactions are transmitted to the nodes in the network. If a mining node happens to compare the two, it discovers that double spend occurs. Then it will not put them in a block. If the transactions do not enter a block, they do not enter the blockchain. Neither of them becomes fact. The bitcoin is not spent.

If one transaction goes into a block and the second arrives later, the second will be regarded as invalid by the miner.

If the block containing one transaction is mined, it goes onto the blockchain. As the blockchain lengthens, it gets broadcasted to the community. Nodes will see that the bitcoin has been spent and they will reject the second transaction.

If the second transaction is also mined by another mining node, then the block goes onto the blockchain, creating fork, since it is inconsistent with the branch that has the block that contains the first transaction.

Now, a couple of features of the protocol ensures an almost certain outcome from such a scenario:

- The creation of a block is via Proof-of-Work. This is a computationally hard problem effectively, and the mining node needs to use raw computing power and time to mine blocks.
- The protocol tells a node to regard the longest fork in the blockchain as the correct one.

Thus, a fork that lengthens quickly attracts nodes that regard it as the correct one. This includes mining nodes. Thereafter, the miner will add to this fork and it lengthens ahead of others. It becomes increasingly harder for other forks to overtake the one that has quickly attracted nodes that regard it to be the correct version of transactional facts.

Both the computational difficulty of the Proof-of-Work algorithm and the moderate pace of block creation (1 block per 10 minutes on average) help to ensure that there is a single branch in the blockchain that is the correct one.

1.2.4 *Proof-of-Work as Consensus Mechanism*

Consensus mechanisms can be understood in an intuitive setting: in a group of people, how can we come to an agreement?

Common solutions are veto power (associated with centralized control) and voting. However, in a distributed network, voting opens the network up for Sybil attacks — the creation of fictitious identities to sway votes in a certain direction.

Bitcoin uses the Proof-of-Work consensus mechanism to achieve Byzantine fault tolerance in networks (i.e., the network is able to come to agreement on its state stably).

What that means is that, in order for a fact to be established (e.g. fact that so-and-so transaction has really occurred), computational power is required. A mining computer has to solve a puzzle that has no shortcut, and solutions must be attempted one-by-one until the correct one is found. Once a miner publishes the result to the puzzle, everyone knows that computational power has been expended in the search and thereby accept the transactions associated to the mining process.

Other than Proof-of-Work, there are other consensus mechanisms available for achieving Byzantine fault tolerance in networks. For example, in Practical Byzantine Fault Tolerance (PBFT), each node publishes a public key, so that any message coming through the node is signed by the node to verify it. Once enough responses that are identical are reached, then we can agree that is a valid transaction. Thus, instead of harnessing computational power to establish the validity of transactions, the sheer number of nodes in agreement is used.

1.3 Scalability Challenges and Potential Solutions

Let us consider issues of scalability from Bitcoin's perspective. The following are potential bottlenecks in Bitcoin's processing capability:

- The heartbeat of the network (i.e., the speed at which a block is added to the blockchain) is 1 per 10 minutes
- Each block of transactions is limited to 1MB in size

- Number of bitcoins and smallest units
- The ever-increasing blockchain size (320 GB in February 2021)

We will look at these issues in turn.

1.3.1 *The 10-Minute Heartbeat*

Bitcoin allows a block to be solved about once every 10 minutes. This is the nature of the heartbeat. To understand how this works, we will need to understand the mining process in more depth.

Individual nodes send out transactions. They are transmitted to neighboring nodes. Each full node verifies these transactions according to a list of criteria. Each mining node aggregates these transactions and attempts to solve a computationally hard puzzle called the Proof-of-Work algorithm. The purpose of the hard puzzle is to slow down the rate at which blocks can go onto the blockchain so that the network comes to a consensus or agreement about the state of the blockchain. This is achieved by getting a node to accept the longest chain in the blockchain (which can have forks) to be the correct state of the system.

The hard puzzle is created by the network. It is of the nature that the only way to solve the puzzle is through sheer computational power — you just have to keep testing a sequence of possible answers for the correct one. When the puzzle is solved, the successful miner broadcasts the block to the network. Nodes may verify that the solution is correct and they will add the block to their respective blockchains.

Each block consists of a block header and a list of transactions that have been accumulated by the miner, together with a generation transaction that awards him with newly minted bitcoins if he were to successfully mine it.

The header is associated with a parameter known as a nonce. The "nonce" for a bitcoin block is a 32-bit (a string of 0s and 1s of length 32) field whose value is set so that the hash of the block will contain a run of leading zeros.

A hash is a function that maps the header into a fixed-length string. Bitcoin uses the particular hashing function called the SHA-256 whose output is a 256-bit (i.e., 32 byte) string.[3]

The puzzle is this: find a nonce that causes the hash of the header to be a 256-bit number that is lower than a particular target. The smaller the target, the harder it is to find such a nonce. And conversely, the larger the target, the easier it is to find such a nonce.

When a nonce is successfully found, the entire block is transmitted to the network. All nodes can run SHA-256 to see for themselves that the hash falls below the targeted number of zeros.

The Bitcoin heartbeat is hard-coded into the client software. It is controlled by what is called the *difficulty* which is a network global parameter. The difficulty is readjusted every 2,016 blocks. It is roughly given by the following formula:

$$\text{current\_difficulty} = \text{old\_difficulty}$$
$$\times (2 \text{ weeks})/(\text{time the past 2,015 blocks took})$$

Hence, if it has taken a shorter time to process the last 2,015 blocks, the current_difficulty will raise, and vice versa.

The target is then computed from the formula:

$$\text{current\_target} = \text{difficulty\_1\_target}/\text{difficulty}$$

where difficulty_1_target is some constant the does not depend on the mining speed.

One way to increase Bitcoin's throughput is to hasten the heartbeat. However, each major change to the code involves major decisions that are usually discussed throughout the community, with developers having perhaps a slightly louder voice. Major changes can split the community and weaken the value of the coin.

Other cryptocurrencies have taken different routes to increase processing speeds. Ripple, which aims to provide solutions for the

---

[3]You may try the SHA-256 function at http://www.xorbin.com/tools/sha256-hash-calculator

banking industry, has a heartbeat of 1 block per 3.5 seconds. Ethereum has a heartbeat of 1 block per 14 seconds. These variations are due to how the consensus is achieved in each case.

1.3.2   The Limit of 1MB

The Bitcoin community discussed the scalability question during the early years of its life. Amidst the disagreements, the Bitcoin Cash hard fork took place in 2017.

Some key ideas behind the splits included:

- Bitcoin Classic: proposed to increase the block size to 2MB
- Bitcoin Unlimited: proposed to have no limit to the block size; rather, the size is to be a settable parameter
- Bitcoin Core: proposed a solution called SegWit

Having no limit to the block size while keeping the 10-minute heartbeat means that miners will be able to process transactions at a faster rate. This favors a small group of miners as mining in Bitcoin has advanced to such a stage that only those who can afford specialized equipment (ASICs) can successfully mine for bitcoins. As it is, mining is currently largely restricted to a small number of mining pools distributed around the world.

SegWit is the process where blocks are made smaller by removing signature data from Bitcoin transactions. In this way, capacity is freed up to add more transactions. Witnesses refer to the transaction signatures. Seg means segregate or to separate them out from the blocks. This solution does not favor miners over ordinary users in its outcome.

Although there have been more spinoffs since Bitcoin Cash, and other cryptocurrencies such as Litecoin have attempted to address the scalability issue, the original bitcoin design of 1MB remains unchanged and bitcoin is still dominant compared to its many forked spinoff tokens.

1.3.3   Number of Bitcoins and Smallest Units

There will eventually be a little bit less than 21 million bitcoins in total as it is hardwired into the code. Each block entitles the miner to earn a number of bitcoins. This is how bitcoin supply is introduced. The award is halved every four years.

It started with 50 BTC per block. This was halved to 25 on November 28, 2012. It is currently 6.25 per block. And it will last this way until 2024–2025.

As the smallest unit that is recognized by the network is 1 satoshi, and 1 BTC is equal to 100 million satoshis; eventually, there will be a total of about 21×10^{14} satoshis in the system.

A sizable fraction of this is expected to be lost by various means. Arguments about whether such a finite state of money supply is good or bad belongs to the realm of economic theorizing.

1.3.4 *Ever-increasing Blockchain*

A complete download of the blockchain from scratch took several days on a Linux laptop. It amounted to 320 GB of data (Figure 1.2).

As the blockchain is meant to live forever as public data, this size will become an issue. If ordinary users are expected to have to download the complete blockchain in order to use the coin, they will be put off.

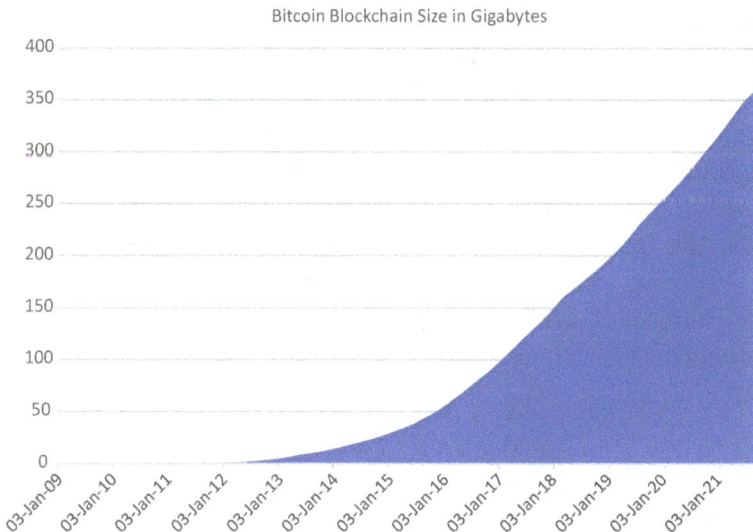

Figure 1.2: Bitcoin blockchain size at 320GB in February 2021.

One way around this is to use the Simplified Payment Verification (SPV) mode. In the SPV mode, clients connect to a full node and download only the block headers. They verify that the headers chain together correctly. They then request information pertaining to payment-related transactions from the remote node, which then provides copies of those transactions along with a Merkle branch linking them to the block where these transactions appear. A Merkle tree, from which the branch derives, is a data structure used for efficiently summarizing and verifying the integrity of large sets of data.

In summary, SPV, with the aid of the Merkle tree for summarizing the data, is the solution to the ever-increasing blockchain in the future. It only requires certain full nodes to carry the complete blockchain.

1.4   Consensus Mechanisms

Consensus mechanisms are means by which a P2P network may achieve consensus on the state of the system. They are used to allow a network to withstand Byzantine faults, i.e., the possibility that faulty or malicious nodes in the network may destroy the ability of the nodes to come to consensus on a system state.

There have been theoretical proposals of consensus mechanisms in the academic literature before Bitcoin. Bitcoin's solution — Satoshi Nakamoto's innovation — uses Proof-of-Work, in which the solution of a computationally hard problem is used to make the network robust to Byzantine faults. That Bitcoin is a fully functional network out on the Internet for almost a decade is an empirical proof that this particular consensus mechanism works in a totally open setting.

A variety of consensus mechanisms have arisen with other cryptocurrency systems. Several that have been considered or are already in place are:

(1) Bitcoin's Proof-of-Work
(2) Monero's Proof-of-Stake
(3) IOTA's Tangle Protocol

We will focus on the Bitcoin's Proof-of-Work in this chapter.

1.4.1   *Proof-of-Work*

In the Bitcoin protocol, a client will take the longest chain in the blockchain to be the correct chain of transactions in the history of the network evolution.

Note that the term "blockchain" here refers to all blocks that have been mined. These blocks do not simply form a linear chain structure. There are branches formed sporadically. However, as the protocol dictates that a client selects the longest chain to be correct, miners — if they follow the protocol — will converge to a single longest chain as they choose one to extend with blocks while ignoring others.

There are several points to highlight here:

(1) Blocks that have been mined and do not have parents are known as orphaned blocks. If they have parents but are not part of the best blockchain, they are to be stale.

(2) The Value Overflow incident caused a major and biggest fork in Bitcoin's history. It was due to an inconsistency in two successive versions of the client.

(3) Malicious miners can be in cahoots to create an alternative longest branch. They will have to overtake the normal longest branch that is created by honest users (commonly called the 51% attack — you will see why in a moment).

Let us consider point (3) more carefully in order to appreciate how things work out.

If a malicious user wishes to attack the system by creating a longest chain, the best he can do is to transmit new transactions involving his own unspents so as to double spend, and to verify these new transactions by extending the blocks in a different way. He will not be able to affect transactions that have been transmitted by other users.

So we consider two chains — one constructed by honest nodes, while the other by the attacher. Let us regard the process of block extensions to be a Binomial random walk, i.e. the successful event is that the honest chain is extended by one block. The failure event is that the attacker's chain is extended by one block. Let the success probability be p and the failure probability be $q = 1 - p$.

Suppose that currently the attacker's chain has length M and the honest chain has length N. The attacker wishes to overtake by growing his chain to be longer than the honest chain.

The probability that the attacker will ever catch up is given by

$$1$$

if $q \geq p$, otherwise it is

$$\left(\frac{p}{q}\right)^{N-M}$$

This formula is quoted from standard results — the problem here is classically known as the Gambler's Ruin.

If $p > q$, we see that the probability that the attacker will catch up decreases exponentially as the length of the honest chain grows beyond the length of his chain.

In the scheme at large, the probability p is determined by the number of honest miners relative to the number of malicious miners. The rate at which blocks are produced is controlled by the protocol to be at about 1 per 10 minutes. This rate is controlled by the difficulty, which is adjusted every 2,016 blocks by using the time to block creation. There is no way to hack this except perhaps by a hard fork in which the code is altered. However, this also requires users to be willing to adopt the new software. As the rule is largely deemed to be fair by users, it is a rock-hard assumption.

Thus, the only way to gain an upper hand in block extension this way is by garnering computational power. For malicious users in cahoots, they will have to have a 51% combined computational power in order to overtake the honest branch with certainty. Otherwise, it is quite unlikely that they will succeed by the Gambler's Ruin argument above.

Let us further consider the issue. When a transaction is submitted and enters the blockchain via a block, the user cannot be at first sure that another chain will arise to overtake the current one in which his transaction is found.

So suppose Alice sends 5 bitcoins to Bob and Bob is required to send some bushels of wheat to Alice in return. He should not do so immediately, because another chain of blocks may arise to overtake the one that contains his transaction, which will nullify the fact that he owns the 5 bitcoins to the community.

However if he finds that his transaction is in a block that has been extended several times, then by the argument above, he will feel safer that the transaction will remain as fact for the community forever.

So the question is, how many blocks must be above his before he feels safe? Suppose this number is z. For the malicious user to change the transaction, he needs to minimally alter the history from the block that is at present z blocks below the blockchain height. Bob does not know much many blocks the malicious Alice has already created as alternative. Let us say the number is k. The probability that this is so, i.e., Alice manages to create k blocks is given by the Poisson process with rate

$$\lambda = z\frac{q}{p}$$

Here, we are assuming that the z blocks created by honest miners are at the average rate. Since the probability that an honest miner creates a block is p while it is q for a malicious user, the expected number of blocks over this same period of time that Alice can create is given by this value of λ.

Hence, the probability that Alice can catch up at this point and she has created k blocks over the same time that honest users create the z blocks is

$$\frac{\lambda^k e^{-\lambda}}{k!} \times \left(\frac{q}{p}\right)^{z-k}$$

if $k \leq z$, and is

$$\frac{\lambda^k e^{-\lambda}}{k!}$$

if $k > z$.

```
import math
q = 0.3
p = 1 - q
for z in range(0, 11):
    s = 1
    l = z * q / p
    for k in range(z + 1):
        s -= l**k * math.exp(- l) / math.factorial(k) * (1 -
  (q / p)**(z - k))
    print z, s
```

Figure 1.3: Python codes computing the probability (body text font size 12).

The overall probability that Alice can catch up is thus

$$1 - \sum_{k=0}^{z} \frac{\lambda^k e^{-\lambda}}{k!} \left(1 - \left(\frac{q}{p}\right)^{z-k}\right)$$

We may work out what this probability is for various values of q and z.

If we use the Python code in Figure 1.3 to do the computation, it can be seen that if malicious blocks are extended with probability 0.3 and honest blocks are extended with probability 0.7, then the probability that a 6 block ahead situation can be overtaken is 0.132111168714.

The 6 block rule is a common guideline for bitcoin users — wait for your transaction to be below 6 blocks before taking it to be permanent.

1.4.2   *Network Integrity, Propagation Delay and Block Creation Speed*

It is important to realize that various pertinent network parameters may be related to each other. The system is complex so that one factor is related to another and they are all tightly bound together. This is the case for the Proof-of-Work consensus protocol, the 10-minute block creation interval, and the block propagation delay in the network.

Propagation delay refers to the fact that the nodes are globally distributed on the Internet and there is a necessary delay in the transmission of data from node to node. This is also affected by the bandwidth of physical channels in-between.

Suppose the block size is increased as in the proposal by Bitcoin Unlimited. The consequence is that the delay will be increased. This means that the time between when a block is first mined to when all nodes receive notification of it will go up. Similarly, if transactions are hashed instead of stored in full, the sizes of blocks will decrease and if left thus, the propagation speed will likewise increase.

What has this got to do with network integrity? Network integrity here refers to the proper maintenance of its key functionality — a longest blockchain that is common to all nodes. If propagation is fast and creation is slow, then each new block that is created is safely added to the blockchain by all nodes. If these two parameters — propagation speed and creation speed — are tweaked, then a less-than-ideal situation may arise.

Suppose propagation is slowed and creation is hastened. What then ensues is that it may be possible for two blocks to be mined within an interval during which the nodes have not had time to update themselves uniformly of the existence of one or the other. Thus one of the blocks will be attached to a parent for some nodes while the other will be attached to the same parent for other nodes. When they communicate and aggregate the information, they will end up with conflicting blocks extending the blockchain.

Ultimately, one of these blocks will be discarded when the longest blockchain pulls away from it. The effort that is expended will be wasted for the community as a whole. The situation is thus not ideal.

On the other hand, it is good to be able to shorten the waiting time between blocks being mined. Merchants generally will not be able to wait for 10 minutes before proceeding with transactions. Most will accept with faith immediately, reasoning that statistically, things will be alright for most small-item transactions.

1.5   Regulatory Challenges

Governments generally protect their rights to the issuance of money. Hence they naturally view Bitcoin and other cryptocurrencies with suspicion. The concerns of governments are:

- The loss of tax revenue
- Money laundering
- Scams and frauds

The current cryptocurrency wave persists largely due to the P2P nature of the network. All nodes on the Internet contain the same data. It is impossible to shut it down by closing any single node. Furthermore, the software code is protected by open-source licenses, which ensures that the code cannot be taken away from public access.

The attitude toward Bitcoin by various countries vary. Singapore regards it to be a purely commercial decision whether businesses want to adopt Bitcoin or not. While in China, financial institutions are not allowed to facilitate bitcoin transactions. Cryptocurrency exchanges and trading platforms are also banned.

In US, different agencies treat the matter differently. The US Treasury classifies bitcoin as a convertible decentralized virtual currency. The Commodity Futures Trading Commission (CFTC) classifies bitcoin as a commodity. The Inland Revenue Service (IRS) requires that bitcoin be taxed as a property.

Ethereum has been careful to emphasize the smart contract service that its platform can provide. This appears to present it in a better light in the eyes of the authority.

With regards to blockchains, Cermeño (2016) highlighted a few regulatory challenges in getting blockchains to be used in the highly regulated financial industry:

(1) Legal framework concerning the legal nature of blockchains and shared distributed ledgers
(2) Legal framework for recognizing blockchains as tamper-proof and immutable nodes
(3) Regulation of the "right to be forgotten"
(4) Legal framework for the validity of documents stored on blockchains as existence or possession evidence

(5) Legal framework for the validity of blockchain issued financial instruments
(6) Legal framework for smart contracts
(7) Regulation of the blockchain as a valid regulatory Internet of Things registry

One thing to note is that, before the legal framework is established, activities such as payments, lending, and investing on the blockchain can (and should) still be regulated. In other words, regulation such as Know Your Customer (KYC) and anti-money laundering (AML) regulation, capital markets regulation, and lending regulation, should still apply.

References

Cermeño, J. S. (2016). BBVA Research: Blockchain in financial services: Regulatory landscape and future challenges for its commercial application. Retrieved from https://www.bbvaresearch.com/wp-content/uploads/2016/12/WP_16-20.pdf (Accessed 5 August 2021).

Murphy, H. (2017). Database move gives blockchain its first big test case. Retrieved from https://www.ft.com/content/aeb63b96-d64b-11e6-944b-e7eb37a6aa8e (Accessed 5 August 2021).

Nakamoto, S. (2008). Bitcoin: A Peer-to-Peer Electronic Cash System. Retrieved from https://bitcoin.org/bitcoin.pdf (Accessed 5 August 2021).

Plan B (2019). Bitcoin: Modeling Bitcoin Value with Scarcity. Retrieved from https://medium.com/@100trillionUSD/modeling-bitcoins-value-with-scarcity-91fa0fc03e25 (Accessed 5 August 2021).

TP ICAP (2021). TP ICAP To Launch Cryptoasset Trading Platform In Collaboration With Fidelity Digital Assets, Zodia Custody And Flow Traders. Press release, 29 June 2021. Retrieved from https://tpicap.com/tpicap/media/press-releases/2021/tp-icap-launch-cryptoasset-trading-platform-collaboration-fidelity (Accessed 5 August 2021).

Wong, J. I. and Kar, I. (2016). Everything you need to know about the Ethereum "hard fork." Retrieved from https://qz.com/730004/everything-you-need-to-know-about-the-ethereum-hard-fork/ (Accessed 5 August 2021).

Chapter 2

The Evolution of Blockchains

Tan Chong Hui

The Bitcoin protocol, which surfaced in 2008–2009, brought together several ideas and technologies, thereby creating a social phenomenon. The underlying protocol, implemented in software form as the Bitcoin node server and client that is downloadable for all, enforces trust in the system through cryptographic means, even though participants who interact to exchange tokens may not trust one another.

It has been about 10 years since the advent of Bitcoin, at the time of writing. Its internals have been dissected and the components tweaked and put together again in different forms. This is possible because the Bitcoin software is under the open-source license.

The most obvious application is to reinvent cryptocurrencies in another form. There are over 4,000 known cryptocurrencies as of early 2021. Table 2.1 shows the top cryptocurrencies in order of market capitalization (Coinmarketcap, 2021). The composition of the list changes frequently, with relative stability at the top.

In the above list, Ethereum stands out for being the platform that aims to generalize the application of the underlying component technologies. Ethereum is not merely a cryptocurrency. It is a smart contract platform. This means that users may write programs to behave like contracts that reside on the network. The contracts can be designed in such a way that they will be enforced on the participants who had agreed to enter into it in the first place. All contractual

Table 2.1:   The top cryptocurrencies by market cap.

Name	Market Capitalization*
Bitcoin	886,166,322,107
Ethereum	170,353,372,337
Cardano	41,590,846,227
Binance Coin	35,544,956,887
Tether	34,988,376,086
Polkadot	32,070,699,961
XRP	20,383,021,276
Litecoin	11,710,781,024
Chainlink	10,733,179,587
Stellar	10,142,997,716

*Market cap in US$, as of February 27, 2021.
Source: Coinmarketcap (2021).

processes will be carried out automatically through computation, which at a deeper level, is the responsibility of the miners to validate.

Blockchain applications such as smart contracts are promising in their potential to disrupt industries. The technology allows records to be stored in such a way that is highly visible to all who are involved, and no one has an absolute say in the contents of the records. Instead, everyone who has a stake has a say in it. This seemingly technical condition actually underlies many transactions involving record keeping in the industry. Bitcoin itself is a case in point — people are trading it as an item of value, mostly unaware of the underlying reality of multi-agent transactional recording keeping that enables it.

Forward-looking industry watchers thus surmise that there will be more to come. It is possible to divide the phases of development into three parts:

- Blockchain 1.0: Cryptocurrencies;
- Blockchain 2.0: Contracts and Decentralized Apps; and
- Blockchain 3.0: Further and Deeper Social Applications (i.e. widespread use of the blockchain technology).

We will discuss these three phases in the remaining sections.

2.1 Blockchain 1.0 — Currency

The advent of bitcoin as a cryptocurrency can be separated into phases. First, the protocol itself is a method or an algorithm to solve the double-spend problem and the Byzantine Generals problem in a system of computer nodes that is found on the Internet. The double-spend problem is that someone can spend the same coin that he has twice. This defeats the idea of value. Bitcoin solves it by specifying that the first transaction to be entered into the blockchain will be regarded as the authoritative one. In other words, the first spend of a coin that is recorded will be taken as the correct one.

The Byzantine Generals problem concerns how a network of nodes may come to a consensual agreement about the state of the system. For Bitcoin, the state of the system is the blockchain itself, which contains all transactions that have been verified. To maintain the blockchain as the system state that is consensually accepted by all participants despite the possibility of breakdowns in the nodes, errors in the messages transmitted, or even the existence of malicious users who may attempt to sabotage the network, Bitcoin implements the Proof-of-Work protocol, which requires many steps of computations before a block of transactions may be verified before it goes onto the blockchain. Miners are incentivized to execute the Proof-of-Work because its successful verification earns them credit in the network in the form of bitcoins.

Initially, the network was in a phase where users were encouraged to participate through mining or those who already have bitcoins gave them away for free. For those who were not designing the system, or who did not pause to think about where it was heading, much of it was plain fun. Such trivialities include an exchange involving BTC 10,000 for 2 Papa John's pizzas. Today, they would be worth almost US$30 million. The significance of such exchanges with tangible things outside of the Bitcoin network enables bitcoins to be compared with the value of real tangible things, which eventually leads to bitcoins themselves acquiring value.

Over the years from 2010 to 2021, cryptocurrency exchanges, payment services, and a host of intermediaries arose. This phase, which we call Blockchain 1.0, also saw software developers being drawn to the underlying and associated technologies. The central concern here is the currency. Some of the strong developers break out of the Bitcoin mold by taking apart its components, arguing for better design, reconfiguring the components, and putting them back together again into other cryptocurrencies.

2.1.1   *Bitcoin*

This is the beginning of the whole phenomenon. The price against the US$ has recently (Feb 2021) peaked at US$47,000 for 1 bitcoin. It still is the biggest showpiece in the space of the new FinTech, cryptocurrencies, and blockchain by sheer size of its market capitalization, maturity of its software and network, as well as its robustness against forks and attacks.

The underlying blockchain technology can be used to carry messages. However, the developers and community have no wish to change the ethos of the project. In other words, they do not wish to expand Bitcoin to include the functioning of smart contracts.

A hot issue facing the Bitcoin community several years ago was an impending fork. With much attention and high usage, the network is being weighed down by the higher transaction volumes. The community is searching for ways to allow the network to process at higher bandwidths. Two camps have arisen from within the community — those who favor the possibility to set a variable block size which requires a hard fork (i.e. significant software changes) and those who favor tweaking the software slightly by changing how transactions are stored, hoping that the better housekeeping can create more space for more transactions. The first camp is known as Bitcoin Unlimited while the latter is known as Bitcoin Core. Those who occupy a middle ground are called Bitcoin Classic — they advocate the blocksize of 2MB (which raises the current 1MB but does not allow arbitrary setting of its size). Whatever the outcome, the scaling problem is real and needs to be tackled. The impending fork will test the community. The value of bitcoin ultimately lies in the stability of the community. The fork will be a good show of its strength.

2.1.2 *Ethereum and Ethereum Classic*

Ethereum is more correctly described as the Ethereum platform. Its inventor Vitalik Buterin proposed that Bitcoin be expanded to allow for programming of smart contracts but was rejected. He then took his idea elsewhere and founded Ethereum. The Ethereum platform promises to be similar to Bitcoin with regard to its foundations — the existence of a currency, the ether, and miners who are incentivized to mine for ethers, which effectively means that they are maintaining the network for the benefit of all other users, the creation of new ether for these miners and gas or transaction fees for them. In addition, this underlying system is supposed to support the creation of smart contracts and decentralized apps. Decentralized apps are collections of smart contracts and other codes that are supposed to achieve certain goals with its users that involve the exchange of tokens and information.

Ethereum is the second largest cryptocurrency in terms of market capitalization. In February 2021, it was priced at US$1,470 per ether. A hacker who stole ethers forced the decision to hard-fork the project in 2016. Linux Foundation' Hyperledger Project created a similar technology for use by the industry. These mark some of the most significant events to date in related space. The hacking event occurred in 2016. A vote was taken and the majority of the decision making body decided to change the code in order to return the money to its original owner. This meant that the blockchain will be altered. However, a small minority revolted, saying that the blockchain must never be tampered with. This led to a hard fork. The majority changed the code and created a new project. The minority continued to further the original project. Miners took sides or contributed to both. As long as there are participants to maintain the networks, they will continue to thrive. Ethereum, which ranks second in the list of market-cap cryptocurrencies, is the majority group led by Vitalik Buterin. The minority group that led the breakaway, now known as Ethereum Classic, inherits a network that contains the intact history of the hacking incident.

The implication of the fork is interesting. At the point of the split, there were two networks. Account holders suddenly find themselves holding on to two copies of ethers, one copy from each network. They could take profit there and then. However, there was also some initial confusion. As the codes were identical at the point of the fork, an ether on one network could be accepted by the other network. Others have commented that, while cryptocurrency protocols are designed to solve the double-spend problem, the problem surfaces in an unexpectedly different guise in the form of forks.

2.2   Blockchain

Different people generalize the Bitcoin concept to create their own cryptocurrency systems with various additions or modifications to the same set of basic features. Ethereum aims to have a general platform that houses all these systems. In particular, its goal to be a platform for the delivery of smart contracts can be regarded as the second wave in the Blockchain movement.

The inventor of Bitcoin, Satoshi Nakamoto, had already anticipated the further development of blockchains in his communication with others in 2010, when he said that "the design supports a tremendous variety of possible transaction types ... Escrow transactions, bonded contracts, their-party arbitration, multiparty signature, etc."

A list of blockchain applications compiled by Ledra Capital in its Mega Master Blockchain List is provided in Table 2.2.

Table 2.2:   The Mega Master Blockchain List.

Categories	Examples
Financial instruments, records and models	Currency, Public and private equities, Bonds
Public records	Land titles, Passports, Votes
Private records	Contracts, Signatures, Wills
Other semi-public records	Certifications, Learning outcomes, Grades
Physical asset keys	Car keys, Hotel room keys, Safety deposit box keys
Intangibles	Coupons, Vouchers, Patents
Others	Documentary records, Nuclear launch codes, GPS network identity

Source: Ledra Capital (2013).

The range of potential applications is broad as the technology is fundamental. The idea is that if it involves records and human agreements, blockchain technology has the potential to reconfigure existing practices in a way that is more efficient or more cost-effective, or simply in a way that disrupts the existing practices. Below is a more detailed description of selected applications in the Blockchain 2.0 space.

2.2.1 *Financial Services*

Ripple by Ripple Labs is using the blockchain technology to impact the banking sector and hence financial services at large. Like Ethereum, it offers the ability to write smart contracts with a language of its invention, called Codius. After the debacle of Mt. Gox, cryptocurrency exchanges are stabilizing and on the rise again. Coinbase is a prime example in this space. PayPal and other traditional online payment services have been or are gradually incorporating bitcoin and other major cryptocurrencies into their payment systems.

2.2.2 *Crowdfunding*

Crowdfunding platforms like Kickstarter and Swarm raise funds for projects. They naturally need to deal with the flow of funds and accounts. The use of cryptocurrencies is a more natural fit compared to traditional monies due to the online nature of these operations.

2.2.3 *Prediction Markets*

In the Bitcoin space, the two foremost prediction markets that are based on bitcoins are Predictious and Fairlay. Conventional prediction markets such as PredictIt, iPredict, and Iowa Electronic Markets are not based on cryptocurrencies as they were established before 2008. The advent of cryptocurrencies naturally intrudes into this space. Internet participation in these markets makes a cryptocurrency-based market more natural and efficient.

2.2.4 *Smart Property*

The idea of a smart property is to transact properties through blockchain-based technology. It works as follows. First an asset is registered in the blockchain. That is, it has a public/private key attached to it. Ownership is regarded to be the possession of the private key. By transferring the private key, the owners transfer the ownership to someone else. A smart contract automates this transaction via code that functions contingent to events. In other words, a smart contract is a program that resides on the blockchain. Its job is to transfer private keys representing possession of assets from one individual to another.

Smart contracts can potentially reduce litigations due to contract disputes that may arise in reality at any point in the contracting process. Automated enforcement agreements remove these potentialities.

2.2.5 *From Smart Contracts to DApps, DAOs, DACs, DASs*

DApps, DAOs, DACs and DASs stand respectively for decentralized apps, decentralized autonomous organizations, decentralized autonomous corporations, decentralized autonomous societies. The thinking is this: societies are made up of corporations and smaller social groups of various kinds, each bounded together through contracts. The use of smart contracts can potentially introduce automation and algorithmic control of these structures. DApps are the starting point of this process. These are applications that live on the blockchain. They effect the exchange of information and funds in the form of cryptocurrencies. Contracts, organizations, and societies consist of DApps that are bundled together.

2.3 Blockchain 3.0

Blockchain technology can potentially reconfigure, not just financial transactions and markets, but also all industries, and ultimately all areas of human endeavor. This phase of the development — Blockchain 3.0 — is still in the state of fathoming. Much of the existing infrastructure will remain as they are for the time being.

People need to be familiar with the technology before they begin to use it. Moreover, the technology has to be fused into existing frameworks and infrastructures. Here we explore three aspects — Namecoin, Blockchain Genomics, and Blockchain Governments.

2.3.1 *Namecoin*

Namecoin is one of the first non-currency applications of blockchain technology. Namecoin is a decentralized name server in analogy with domain name service/system (DNS) in the centralized world. The DNS on the Internet is controlled by the Internet Corporation for Assigned Names and Numbers (ICANN). Everyone on the Internet finds each other through this centralized naming service. The database maintained by ICANN, if compromised, can disrupt the functioning of the entire Internet. This suggests the huge power that ICANN wields. Namecoin aims to be an alternative DNS that is not controlled by any government or corporation. In a centralized DNS, authority can exercise censorship by forbidding access to various domains or groups of domains. In a decentralized DNS, as long as the peer-to-peer (P2P) network is maintained by volunteers, domain names in the blockchain will always be accessible.

2.3.2 *Blockchain Genomics*

This refers to having personal genomic data in the public blockchain. The data will be made available to anyone with the appropriate private key. Currently, genomic data is under the control of local governments. There are those who question the authority of having the rights to withhold personal data. Genomic sequencing is a computationally hard problem in which breakthrough can lead to solutions in medicine. Having geonomic data on the blockchain allows for greater participation in the process.

2.3.3 *Blockchain Governments*

Governments may be impacted by blockchains in a way that is beneficial to the community at large. Services may be provided in a more decentralized manner that is at once cheaper, more efficient, and more personalized. For instance, one may imagine along the lines of "choose your government, choose your service." Already, we see the power of the community at work in the decisions on the directions of open-source projects that create the cryptocurrency communities. Cryptocurrencies enable scarce resources like money to be transmitted over the Internet, in addition to information, in a P2P fashion. The state of the network is directed by anyone who has a stake in the community (as spelt out by the consensus protocols, etc.). An example of a governmental service that is impacted by Bitcoin is the occurrence of a marriage[1] in August 2014 that was submitted to the Bitcoin blockchain. The vows were transmitted in the text annotation field, embedded in a Bitcoin transaction, which appear in the blockchain, for good. The couple used a CoinOutlet Bitcoin ATM to initiate a .1 BTC burn transaction. A burn transaction is one that sends bitcoins to an address that renders the bitcoin unusable forever. The transaction that the couple sent contains their wedding vows.

2.4   Blockchains Applications

2.4.1   *Public vs Private Blockchains*

Recall that blockchain is the central data structure of cryptocurrency protocols. It is this data structure that keeps track of the entire history of transactions (in the case of Bitcoin) or balances (in the case of Ethereum) in an unalterable way that allows the networks to acquire a financial significance — wherein participants can transfer tokens to each other, or they can enter into contracts with each other, without having to trust each other directly. The trust is instead relegated to the entire network of users, the protocol and the cryptographic enforcements of signatures, etc. Bitcoin runs on a public blockchain. This means that anyone can leave a record in the blockchain. One may simply download a Bitcoin wallet and send a valid transaction. Then that will become a record in the blockchain.

---

[1]See https://www.ccn.com/bitcoin-wedding-marriage-on-the-blockchain/

Cryptocurrency systems that are in the public domain run on public blockchains in this manner.

Private blockchains restrict access to a selected group of users. Another way to consider private blockchains is that they are public blockchains with functionalities that allow configurations of user access privileges to be set. A prime example of a private blockchain software is Multichain.[2] This is a fork of the Bitcoin project that adds user-access privilege features into the underlying Bitcoin software. We will describe it in detail later.

With user-access privilege features, blockchains can be put on the Internet and at the same allow only a selected group of users to be participants on the blockchain. This may be useful if a small community wishes to issue cryptocurrency to itself for whatever incentive reasons and they only want their affairs to be restricted to themselves. The small community may be an organization of some sort. Another possible scenario is in the initial issuance of shares in a startup. Prior to an IPO, shares may be given out on a private basis. This initially-private-later-public mode can be configured with a private blockchain. Clearly, private blockchains are functionally more useful than a public blockchain since the additional privacy feature can simply be toggled off to make it public.

Considering the fact that blockchain technology enables the tracking of assets in a trust-less fashion, that industries ranging from finance, legal, accountancy to supply chain management are all concerned with tracking of assets in various ways, the ability to configure privacy settings or access privileges in private blockchain technology gives it a lot of potential on the scene.

2.4.2 *Ethereum, Hyperledger, and Multichain*

The original blockchain is that of Bitcoin. Variations have since arisen. We will consider three prominent blockchain variations here: Ethereum, Hyperledger, and Multichain. In the structure of the Bitcoin blockchain (see Figure 2.1), transactions are placed into a

---

[2]See https://www.multichain.com/

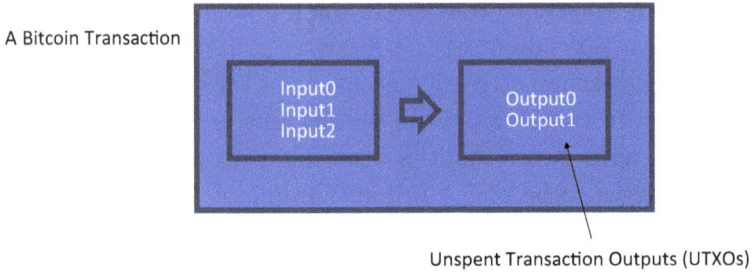

Figure 2.1:   Bitcoin transactions and unspent transaction outputs.

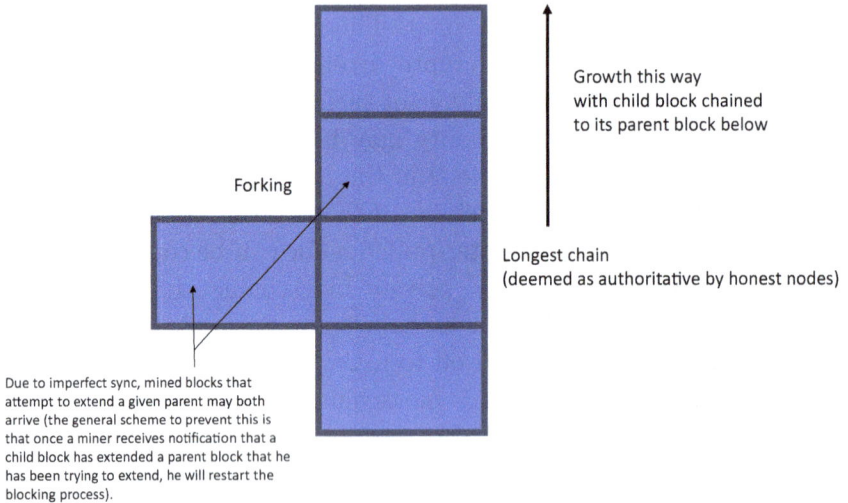

Figure 2.2:   Forking.

block by a miner who succeeds to have his block accepted by peers if he solves the Proof-of-Work problem. Blocks reference earlier blocks in a chain, hence the name blockchain. Two child blocks to a parent block constitute a fork — this can occur if a miner broadcasts a block to extend a parent prior to receiving information from another miner who is also trying to extend the same parent. Forks are resolved by ensuring that nodes select the longest chain as authoritative in the protocol (see Figure 2.2). Anyone can join the network and transact or be a miner.

2.4.2.1 *Ethereum*

The Ethereum blockchain does not store transactions like in Bitcoin. Instead, it contains a list of accounts where each account has a balance, as well as Ethereum-specific data (code and internal storage). A transaction is valid if the sending account has enough balance to pay for it, in which case the sending account is debited and the receiving account is credited with the value. The Ethereum-specific data allows the platform to be able to process smart contracts.

Miners are the ones who insert blocks into the blockchain. However, instead of solving a problem by a computationally intensive hashing algorithm, Ethereum's Proof-of-Work, known as Ethash, is memory-hard. This means that a substantial amount of memory is required in the mining process. Ethereum will soon change to a Proof-of-Stake model of consensus, rendering this moot.

The Ethereum blockchain recognizes and rewards blocks called uncles. These are blocks that do not contribute information content to the blockchain, but are nonetheless regarded to assist in the maintenance of the network. The idea is that, instead of requiring nodes to select the longest chain to be the authoritative one, nodes select the heaviest chain to be the authoritative one. Though an uncle does not contribute to the information in the blockchain, the mining of uncles is rewarded — 7/8 of static block reward (about 4.375 Ether) — with a maximum of 2 uncles allowed per block. It makes this chain heavier and is thus preferred by honest nodes seeking an authoritative chain. Like Bitcoin, Ethereum is a public network (as anyone may join the network and the blockchain is publicly viewable) (Figure 2.3).

2.4.2.2 *Hyperledger*

The Hyperledger is a project of open-source blockchains and associated tools started by Linux Foundation in December 2015. It aims to develop blockchain software as has been surfaced by the cryptocurrency communities. The blockchain technology has taken the world by storm. The Linux Foundation's entry marks the

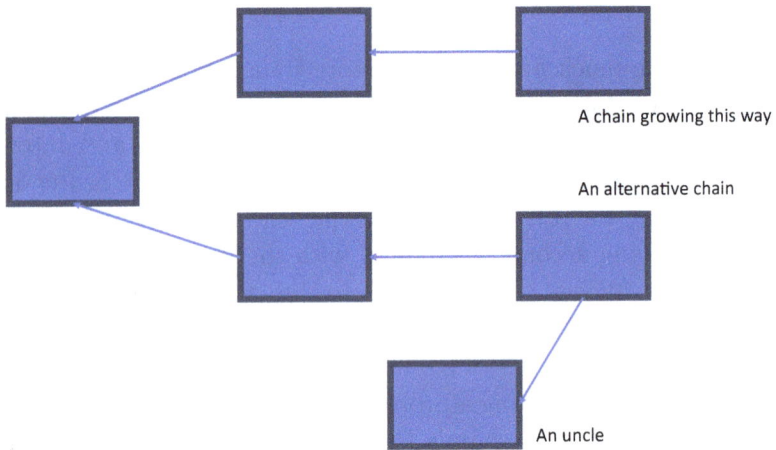

Figure 2.3: Ethereum blockchain.

recognition of the general importance of the technology and a sign to create a level playing infrastructural field for blockchain applications.

The Hyperledger project collaborates with the industry in its work. Its members include well-known technology platform companies and financial services firms. The governance of the project is managed by a governing board comprising 20 members from the Hyperledger membership. IBM, in particular, is an active player here. For instance, it unveiled its "Blockchain as a Service" in March 2017 to provide blockchain solutions to the industry that are built on top of the Hyperledger.

The Hyperledger project currently has five components: Hyperledger Burrow, Hyperledger Fabric, Hyperledger Iroha, Hyperledger Sawtooth and Hyperledger Indy. Hyperledger Burrow is a permissionable smart contract machine built in part to the specification of the Ethereum Virtual Machine. Hyperledger Fabric refers to an implementation of blockchain technology that is intended as a foundation for developing blockchain applications or solutions. Hyperledger Iroha is a distributed ledger project that was designed to be simple and easy to incorporate into infrastructural projects requiring distributed ledger technology. Hyperledger Sawtooth is a modular blockchain suite designed for versatility and scalability. Lastly, Hyperledger Indy provides tools, libraries, and reusable components for interoperable digital identities rooted on blockchains or other distributed ledgers. Details of what the individual component provides can only be appreciated with actual usage — something that belongs to the realm of software developers. Nonetheless, one can glean the overall significance from the brief descriptions.

Here are some high-level points about these components, for instance. The allusion to the Ethereum Virtual Machine in Hyperledger Burrow shows the open-source nature of all these projects. The Ethereum platform runs on the open-source basis. Therefore, its ideas are not proprietary. Linux Foundation's usage is legally sound. Overall, it indicates that the world of blockchains and associated applications will proliferate as we go along.

There will be impacts to the industries as the technology provides alternative solutions to the storage and tracking of records. Particularly for finance, the trend spells impending deep-rooted change to the business of financial intermediation — which is basically what banks, brokers, and exchanges do.

The components of Hyperledger also give a sense of the proliferation of software related to the blockchain. From the extraction of the blockchain from Bitcoin, now, blockchain itself is undergoing transformations in the form of specific usage and the creation of tools to support these specific usages. Burrow is being developed as a smart contract platform. This parallels the goals of Ethereum. Iroha, Sawtooth, and Indy are variations and supporting tools.

The main difference between Hyperledger and Bitcoin or Ethereum is that the "spirit" is missing — Bitcoin and Ethereum support an existing community of users who exchange cryptocurrencies of their networks with real-world goods and services. Hyperledger only has the technology and it can always keep up with whatever technology that the Bitcoin and Ethereum communities come up with. It simply does not have an existing community and hence no preexisting value. Users of the Hyperledger technology will have to create value on their own with it. Table 2.3 summarizes the comparison between Bitcoin, Ethereum, and Hyperledger.

Table 2.3: Comparison between Bitcoin, Ethereum, and Hyperledger.

	Bitcoin	**Ethereum**	**Hyperledger**
Cryptocurrency required	bitcoin	ether, user-created cryptocurrencies	none
Network	public	public or permissioned	permissioned
Transactions	anonymous	anonymous or private	public or confidential
Consensus	Proof-of-Work	Proof-of-Work	Practical Byzantine Fault Tolerance
Smart contracts (business logic)	none	yes (Solidity, Serpent, LLL)	yes (chaincode)
Language	C++	Golang, C++, Python	Golang, Java

Practical Byzantine Fault Tolerance (PBFT) in Hyperledger is an algorithm by Castro and Liskov (2002). The position of PBFT in blockchain systems is parallel to Proof-of-Work in Bitcoin and Ethereum. They are all known as consensus algorithms. Such algorithms are meant to combat Byzantine faults in distributed systems, i.e. nodes that are widely separate and need to communicate with each other to agree on a system state uniformly. In a simple non-Byzantine setting, nodes can fail. In a Byzantine setting, the situation is more dire as malicious nodes may attempt to mislead honest nodes. We have already seen how Proof-of-Work in Bitcoin solves the problem.

In PBFT, the algorithm proceeds in four stages:

(1) A client sends a request to invoke a service operation to the primary;
(2) The primary multicasts the request to the backups;
(3) Replicas execute the request and send a reply to the client;
(4) The client waits for $f + 1$ replies from different replicas with the same result. This is the result of the operation.

Here the client wishes to request for a service operation. Replicas are nodes that replicate the system state and are able to provide the service. A sufficiently large number of identical replies from these replicas is deemed to be the correct answer.

2.4.2.3 *Multichain*

Multichain is a fork of the Bitcoin project that builds in permissions. It claims to help organizations to rapidly build applications on blockchains and shared ledgers. Multichain was created by Gideon Greenspan, the CEO of Coin Sciences. His rationale and design principles are described in Greenspan (2015).

By being a fork of the Bitcoin project, the underlying layer of the software behaves identically to Bitcoin. This helps users familiar with Bitcoin to ease into using Multichain. This is also a key point of difference from Hyperledger. As Hyperledger is not a fork of open-source projects, we do not expect close similarity in code and usage except for similarity in blockchain concepts.

A main difference between Multichain and the other blockchains is its consensus algorithm. Multichain uses a round-robin method of establishing global consensus. A group of users is designated to be miners by the superuser. A parameter known as mining diversity enforces that each miner cannot contribute to blocks that are too close together on the blockchain. This enforces that the blockchain is created collectively by the miners with each miner having a part to play.

In Multichain, transaction fees and block rewards are set to zero by default. Computationally difficult Proof of-Work in the sense of Bitcoin is absent. Miners contribute blocks to uphold the diversity of stakeholders in the functioning network. The miner status itself is an indication of stake. Alternatively, miners may charge network participants a fixed annual service fee. These are configurable.

Overall, Multichain allows participants to maintain a database on a mutually consensual basis. The P2P nature implies robustness as the malfunctioning of one server will not affect its continued existence, unlike in a centralized setup. Assets continue to remain under the possession of each participant and do not have to move from hand to hand — which can incur transaction costs in the real world. Moreover, as the control of the blockchain database is in the hands of the miners, no one participant can unilaterally decide which transactions are valid.

2.5   Blockchain Use Cases

Use cases are examples of how the blockchain technology can be used. They can be real or hypothetical. As blockchain is a relatively new technology, uses are still being discovered. Use cases help to map real-world scenarios to underlying concepts and assist in stimulating new ideas for further applications. Here, we review three use cases from Ethereum, Hyperledger, and Multichain, respectively.

2.5.1   *Ethereum Use Cases*

Ethereum use cases are in the form of smart contracts or DApps created to solve real-world problems or to offer new solutions to existing ones.

Augur is a decentralized prediction market that is built on the Ethereum blockchain. It is prediction tool for real-world events.

vDice is the analog of SatoshiDICE — a "blockchain-based betting game" operating since 2012. By many metrics, SatoshiDICE is still the most successful Bitcoin enterprise to date. vDice Gameplay is a similar application.

EtherOpt is a decentralized options exchange built on Ethereum. The options are vanilla call and put options on the price of Ethereum in US$ as reported by Poloniex and Coindesk and verified by Reality Keys. Poloniex and Coindesk are cryptocurrency exchanges. Reality Keys provides automated and human-verified data designed to enable a new generation of automated, trust-free information services.

Oraclize helps to fetch external data to smart contracts. It is a service that is poised to support the rising smart contract scene on Ethereum.

Digix Global is an asset tokenization service built on Ethereum. It allows users to purchase gold bullion with Bitcoin or Ether.

2.5.2   *Hyperledger Use Cases*

According to a report in *Financial Times* dated March 28, 2017, a commodities trading house (Trafigura) and a bank (Natixis) are testing blockchain as a means for settling deals in the oil market. It is hoped that the technology can ease the cumbersome process of exchanging contracts, letters of credit, inspection, and other paperwork by email or fax when one company sells oil to another. This could also help traders reduce the cost of oil in transit. IBM hosted the test for the two companies. A use case described by the Hyperledger Requirements Working Group focuses on supply-chain traceability through anti-counterfeiting. It is claimed that blockchain's growth in Supply Chain will eclipse that of its growth in FinTech.

Traceability as an issue in supply chain management concerns the accounting of all parts and components in the development of products. The existing situation is a fragmented one. To trace parts and components in the supply chain, one must work through a maze of different vendors, standards, and technologies. Blockchain technology provides a means by which every step in the supply chain can be readily tracked.

2.5.3 *Multichain Use Cases*

A bottleneck in extending the blockchain solution from Bitcoin to other real-world problems is confidentiality. In usual financial transactions, the existence of a trusted financial intermediary plays an important role, the magnitude of which is often glossed over. Data kept by the intermediary is trusted. Conversely, participants in financial transactions trust the intermediary with their data. This is the root foundation for financial flows to occur. As a consequence, financial intermediaries take a sizable cut in commission for their service. Thus, the idea that blockchains can replace financial intermediation completely must be suitably understood, and any highly pegged expectation of its real-world uses must be suitably adjusted.

Multichain's use cases start with this premise and makes it clear what the real strengths of a blockchain is as compared to a traditional centralized database. Blockchains enable multiple parties who do not fully trust each other to safely and directly share a single database without requiring a trusted intermediary. All participants of a blockchain can witness all transactions on the blockchain and no small group of individuals can corrupt the records. In other words, the essential characteristic of a blockchain that distinguishes it from centralized database is that every user is able to read everything but no single user controls who can write what into it. With this understanding, four realistic use cases for Multichain are: (1) lightweight financial systems, (2) provenance tracking, (3) interorganizational record keeping, and (4) multiparty aggregation.

Lightweight financial systems refer to a community that wishes to set up a system of currency or financial instruments that is similar to what we have witnessed for Bitcoin. Multichain can assist a small community to achieve this goal. An example that fits this description is Ithaca Hours. Provenance tracking refers to the tracking of the origin and movement of high-value items in a supply chain. For example, when a luxury good is dispatched from one place to another, a token on the blockchain is created alongside and issued by a trusted party. As the good moves along the supply chain and changes hands, the token moves together with it. The role of the token is to suggest authenticity. This role is traditionally played by printed paper. A paper plus a seal authenticate a good. With blockchain, electronic tokens can replace paper and are hence harder to forge. The permission settings of Multichain facilitates this use case. Interorganizational record keeping refers to the keeping and tracking of records. This use case is similar to provenance tracking, except that the records do not reference anything physical. Multiparty aggregation refers to the need to combine information from a large number of separate sources. Multichain can help to overcome the infrastructure difficulty in doing so. For instance, several banks need to share information to work on a large IPO. One way to do so is to hire a trusted intermediary to manage the data in a centralized fashion. Multichain offers a cheaper alternative. The banks can share their data on the blockchain without fear that others may modify or delete the data.

References

M. Castro and B. Liskov (2002). Practical Byzantine Fault Tolerance and Proactive Recovery. Retrieved from http://www.pmg.csail.mit.edu/papers/bft-tocs.pdf (Accessed 27 May 2021).

Coinmarketcap. (2021). All Cryptocurrencies. Retrieved from coinmarketcap. com (Accessed 27 May 2021).

G. Greenspan (2015). MultiChain Private Blockchain — White Paper. Retrieved from https://www.multichain.com/download/MultiChain-White-Paper.pdf (Accessed 27 May 2021).

Ledra Capital (2013). Bitcoin Series 24: The Mega-Master Blockchain List. Retrieved from http://ledracapital.com/blog/2014/3/11/bitcoin-series-24-the-mega-master-blockchain-list (Accessed 27 May 2021).

Chapter 3

Cryptography and Its Role in Blockchain

Lau Jing Feng

A blockchain is a digital ledger in which transactions are recorded chronologically and publicly. It was not until 2008 that the idea of blockchains was fully developed — someone using the fictitious name Satoshi Nakamoto published a paper titled "Bitcoin: A Peer-to-Peer Electronic Cash System." This paper built on previous work of Hal Finney's reusable Proof-of-Work system. Blockchains have since been applied as digital currencies and as solutions to other problems.

The Bitcoin network was launched in 2009 and was initially used by a small group of cryptographers and hobbyists. Subsequently, Bitcoin was adopted by darknet marketplaces and blockchains started to be practically adopted widely. As the bitcoin cryptocurrency became more popular, many other cryptocurrencies, otherwise known as altcoins, were developed. The more well-known altcoins included Ethereum, Litecoin, and Ripple. Ethereum allowed users to develop apps and come up with smart contracts between parties. Interest in blockchain technology from the public, major companies, and startups subsequently grew.

Even though the price of cryptocurrencies rose and dropped sharply, the number of businesses that accept them are limited. Also, the Bitcoin network cannot handle high transaction volumes similar to Mastercard and Visa. Currently, cryptocurrencies serve as speculative investments or a means to buy illicit products from darknet marketplaces.

Numerous blockchain initiatives apply the technology for use in supply-chain management, financial transactions, smart contracts, and decentralized storage. These include IBM Food Trust and Walmart's foray into adopting blockchains in food supply logistics management, UBS adopting blockchains for financial settlements, and the Australian Stock Exchange adopting blockchains for distributed ledger technology.

The purpose of this expository chapter is to give central concepts of blockchains and how they relate to cryptography.

3.1 Introduction to Cryptography

Cryptography is the practice and study of techniques for secure communication in the presence of third parties called adversaries. Modern cryptography lies in the intersection of mathematics, computer science, electrical engineering, and physics.

If the recipient knows how to convert the coded message back to its original form and adversaries do not, we may assume that the communication is safe. With research and technological advancement, people have significantly improved their code-breaking abilities. Hence, to safeguard our information, we have to use codes that are much more complicated. The design of such complicated codes and algorithms such as AES and RSA involve a lot of mathematics, and these algorithms are implemented in computers for encryption and decryption.

In most data transmission settings, we usually need the following four properties:

- Confidentiality — The ability to keep data hidden from unauthorized parties
- Authentication — The ability to verify that the other party is really who they claim they are and not some imposter or spy.
- Integrity — Retaining the integrity of data means the data has not been altered or tampered by anyone else.

- Non-repudiation — This property means that the individual or entity who was responsible for an action cannot claim that they were not involved.

Encryption algorithms such as AES are used to ensure confidentiality.

There are two major types of encryption:

- Symmetric-key encryption — For this type of encryption, the same key is used to encrypt and decrypt data. This approach is commonly used in cybersecurity. The most prevalent symmetric-key algorithm is AES.
- Public-key (asymmetric) encryption — Public-key cryptography deploys distinct keys for the encryption and decryption processes. The public key is shared openly and the private key is kept confidential. It is based on some interesting mathematical properties and allows two parties who have not met before to exchange information securely. However, this is relatively inefficient compared to symmetric-key encryption.

3.2 The Bitcoin Blockchain

Bitcoin is a cryptography-based currency that is based on a decentralized financial system, in which this value is transferred through a chain of digital signatures that are similar to handwritten signatures and ledgers. We shall focus more on the Bitcoin blockchain as an example to illustrate how cryptography is applied to blockchain technology in general.

3.3 Hashing

Suppose there is an active adversary who is able change the content of messages transmitted between person A and person B. Encryption itself is insufficient to eliminate such threats.

To detect changes made to transmitted messages, we can use a cryptographic hash function in some settings. A hash function is used to make a short "fingerprint" of some data; if the data is changed, then the fingerprint will unlikely be valid. The integrity of the data can be verified constantly by recalculating the fingerprint and checking that the fingerprint has not been modified.

Let h be a hash function and x be some data. Define the corresponding fingerprint by $y = h(x)$. This fingerprint is often called a message digest. Normally, a message digest is a fairly short binary string; 160 bits or 256 bits. y is stored in a secure place but x is not. If x is modified to x', then by ensuring that y is not a message digest for x', we can check whether x has been modified by calculating the message digest $y' = h(x')$ and checking that $y' \neq y$.

The discussion so far assumes the existence of a single fixed hash function. It is also useful to consider a hash family which is a family of keyed hash functions. This family is such that there is a different hash function for each possible key. Keyed hash functions are often used as message authentication codes (MACs).

Suppose A and B share a secret key k which determines a hash function h_k. For a message x, the corresponding authentication tag is $y = h_k(x)$. This tag can be calculated by either A or B. The pair (xy) can be transmitted over an insecure channel from A to B or from B to A. Suppose B receives the pair (xy) from A. Then he verifies whether $y = h_k(x)$ by recalculating the tag. If this equality holds, then assuming the hash family is "secure," B is confident that both x and y are not changed by an adversary and the message x came from A.

The main difference between the assurance of data integrity by an unkeyed hash function versus a keyed hash function is that the message digest of an unkeyed hash function must be securely stored so that it cannot be changed by an adversary whereas the data and the authentication tag can be transmitted over an insecure channel using a keyed hash function securely.

Define a hash family to be a four-tuple $(\mathcal{X}, \mathcal{Y}, \mathcal{K}, \mathcal{H})$ such that the following conditions are satisfied:

- $\mathcal{X}$ is a set of possible messages;
- $\mathcal{Y}$ is a finite set of possible message digests or authentication tags;
- $\mathcal{K}$, the keyspace is a finite set of possible keys;

- For each $k \in \mathcal{K}$, there is a hash function $h_k \in H$. Each h_k: $X \longrightarrow Y$.

For a set S, denote its cardinality by $\text{Card}(S)$. If X is a finite set and $\text{Card}(X) \geq 2\text{Card}(Y)$, we say that h is a compression function. A pair $(x, y) \in X \times Y$ is a valid pair under a hash function h if $h(x) = y$. For a hash function $h : X \to Y$, we say there is a collision if there exists $x, x' \in X$ such that $x \neq x'$ and $h(x) = h(x')$. A hash function where we cannot efficiently find $x, x' \in X$ such that $x \neq x'$ and $h(x) = h(x')$ is said to be collision resistant.

3.3.1 Iterated Hash Functions

We restrict to the case to hash functions whose domain and codomain consists of bitstrings (i.e., strings formed by zeros and ones). Denote the length of a bitstring x by $|x|$ and the concatenation of bitstrings x and y by $x \| y$.

For $t \geq 1$, let $c : \{0, 1\}^{m+t} \longrightarrow \{0, 1\}^m$ be a compression function. We construct an iterated hash function

$$h : \bigcup_{i=m+t+1}^{\infty} \{0, 1\}^i \longrightarrow \{0, 1\}^l$$

using c. Given an input string x where $|x| \geq m + t + 1$, we construct a string y by a public key algorithm such that $|y|$ is divisible by t. This is usually done by setting

$$y = x \| p(x),$$

where $p(x)$ is constructed from x usually by incorporating the value of $|x|$ and lengthens the output by extra bits so the resulting string y has a length which is a multiple of t. Let

$$y = y_1 \| y_2 \| \cdots \| y_r,$$

where $|y_i| = t$ for each $1 \leq i \leq r$. We should ensure that the map $x \to y$ is injective for otherwise it is possible there exist $x' \neq x$ and $y' = y$. Then $h(x') = h(x)$ and h would not be collision resistant. This is known as the preprocessing step.

Let IV be a bitstring of length m which is a public initial value. We perform the following calculation:

$$IV \rightarrow z_0$$
$$c(z_0||y_1) \rightarrow z_1$$
$$c(z_1||y_2) \rightarrow z_2$$
$$\vdots \quad \vdots \quad \vdots$$
$$c(z_{r-1}||y_r) \rightarrow z_r.$$

This is called the processing step.

Let $g : \{0, 1\}^m \rightarrow \{0, 1\}^l$ be a public function. Define

$$h(x) = g(z_r).$$

Many hash functions commonly used in industries are iterated hash functions and are special cases of the generic construction described above as well as the more well-known Merkle–Damgård construction.

Secure Hash Algorithm (a.k.a. SHA-0) was proposed by National Institute of Standards and Technology (a.k.a. NIST in 1993 and adopted as FIPS 180). Subsequently, SHA-1 as a slight modification was issued in 1995 as FIPs 180-1. Hash functions were modified several times to improve the security of the later versions against attacks which were used in earlier versions.

In 2004, Joux reported a collision for SHA-0 at CRYPTO2004 and Stevens, Bursztein, Karpman, Albertini and Markov announced the first collision for SHA-1 on February 23, 2017.

SHA-2 includes four hash functions namely SHA-224, SHA-256, SHA-384 and SHA-512. The suffixes "224," "256," "384," and "512" are the size of the respective message digests of these four hash functions. These hash functions are also iterated hash functions but they are much more complex than SHA-1. SHA-256, SHA-384, and SHA-512 were approved as the FISP standard in 2002.

In the SHA family, the most recent hash functions are the SHA-3 hash functions. These hash functions are based on a method known as the sponge construction.

Cryptographic hash functions have several important features which render them useful.

- Deterministic — A fixed input always has the same output.
- Uniqueness — The likelihood of two distinct inputs having the same output is so low that we do not really worry about it.
- Infeasible to trace back the original input from a given output.
- Hashes can be quickly calculated.
- Slight changes in input results in very different outputs.

The cryptographic hash functions enable us to:

- Show that we have certain data without having to reveal that data.
- Avoid transactions from being changed by adversaries.
- Check transactions without fully knowing a block.
- Reduce the complexity of transactions.
- Create cryptographic puzzles that are part of the blockchain mining process.

These characteristics of hashes are used in the following areas of the Bitcoin blockchain:

- When a transaction is performed, data from previous transactions is hashed and included in the present transaction and current data is also hashed to create a transaction ID which can be utilized to trace the transaction details on the blockchain.
- A hash of the public key is used as the address where users can transfer funds to. This allows the addresses to be more compact and easier to work with and makes transactions more secure.
- As a part of blockchain's Proof-of-Work system.

We now look at how these are applied in a transaction by outlining a simple example.

Suppose A receives 12 bitcoins through three separate transactions. Her bitcoins are retained in the separate amounts that she received from previous transactions. In the first transaction she received three bitcoins, in the second transaction she received four bitcoins, and in the third transaction she received five bitcoins.

A then wants to buy a car from B using 10 bitcoins. She then sends all the 12 bitcoins from the previous transactions to cover the cost and the remaining 2 bitcoins (after subtracting any transaction fee) are returned to her as change. For simplicity, we will assume there is no transaction fee.

A proves that she has ownership of the three separate inputs by using a signature script which is also an unlocking script. This script consists of A's public key and her digital signature. The public key shows the address of the outputs from the previous transactions whereas her digital signature verifies that she is the real owner.

We now provide some technical details of some cryptosystems and digital signature schemes that leads to the development of the elliptic curve digital signature algorithm and Merkle signature scheme which is widely used in blockchain technology.

3.3.2 *Discrete Logarithm*

Let $(G, \bullet)$ be a multiplicative group and $\alpha \in G$ be of order n and β be an element of the subgroup generated by α. Define the discrete logarithm of β with respect to α, $\log_\alpha \beta$ to be the unique integer m, $0 \le m \le n - 1$ such that

$$\alpha^m = \beta.$$

Solving for the discrete logarithm of β with respect to α is known as the Discrete Logarithm problem. Based on the Discrete Logarithm problem of elements in $(\mathbb{Z}/p\mathbb{Z})^*$ where p is a prime, Taher ElGamal (1985) proposed a public-key cryptosystem known as the ElGamal Cryptosystem where it is necessary for the Discrete Logarithm Problem in $(\mathbb{Z}/p\mathbb{Z})^*$ to be computationally infeasible so that the ElGamal Cryptosystem is secure.

We illustrate the algorithm underlying the ElGamal Cryptosystem with a numerical example. Let $p = 2579$ and $\alpha = 2$. Then α is a generator in $(\mathbb{Z}/2579\mathbb{Z})^*$. Let $a = 765$ be the private key so that

$$\beta = 2^{765} \bmod 2579.$$

Suppose A wants to send the message $x = 1299$ to B and she chooses a random integer $k = 853$. She then calculates $y_1 = 2^{853} \equiv$

$949 \bmod 2579$ and

$$y_2 = 1299(949^{853}) \equiv 2396 \bmod 2579.$$

B then receives the ciphertext $y = (435, 2396)$ and calculates

$$x = 2396(435^{765})^{-1} \equiv 1299 \bmod 2579,$$

which was the plaintext A had.

Various other public-key cryptographic algorithms are also developed based on the computational infeasibility of the Discrete Logarithm problem.

3.3.3 *Signature Schemes*

A physical handwritten signature attached to a document is normally used to identify clearly the person responsible for it. A signature scheme is a procedure for signing messages in electronic form. Thus, such a signed message can be sent over a computer network.

There are some significant differences between physical handwritten and digital signatures. For a physical handwritten signature, the signature is part of the signed document but a digital signature is not physically attached to the signed message, so the encryption algorithm should "bind" the signature to the message. Second, physical handwritten signatures are verified by comparing them with other genuine physical handwritten signatures, whereas digital signatures are verified using publicly known verification algorithms. Lastly, a "copy" of a signed digital message is identical to the original signed message but a copy of a signed physical paper document is usually distinguishable from the original.

A signature scheme is a five-tuple $(\mathcal{P}, \mathcal{A}, \mathcal{K}, \mathcal{S}, \mathcal{V})$ satisfying the following conditions:

- $\mathcal{P}$ is a finite set of possible messages.
- $\mathcal{A}$ is a finite set of possible signatures.
- $\mathcal{K}$ is a finite set of possible keys.
- For each $\mathcal{K} \in \mathcal{K}$, there is a signing algorithm $sig_K \in \mathcal{S}$ and a corresponding verification algorithm $ver_K \in \mathcal{V}$. Each $sig_K : \mathcal{P} \to \mathcal{A}$ and $ver_K : \mathcal{P} \times \mathcal{A} \to \{true, false\}$ are functions such that the

following equations is satisfied for every message $x \in \mathcal{P}$ and for every signature $y \in \mathcal{A}$:

$$ver_K(x, y) = \begin{cases} true \ if \ y = sig_K(x) \\ false \ if \ y \neq sig_K(x). \end{cases}$$

A pair (x, y) where $x \in \mathcal{P}$ and $y \in \mathcal{A}$ is called a signed message.

For every $K \in \mathcal{K}$, the functions sig_K and ver_K are supposed to be polynomial-time functions. The signing algorithm sig_K will be private and the verification algorithm ver_K will be public. For a message x, it should be computationally infeasible for people other than the author to calculate a signature y such that $ver_K(x, y) = true$.

3.3.4   *Signatures and Hash Functions*

Signature schemes are usually used together with a secure crypto-graphic hash function. The hash function $h : \{0, 1\}^* \to \mathcal{Z}$ will take a message of arbitrary length and outputs a message digest of pre-fixed size. The message digest is then signed with a signature scheme $(\mathcal{P}, \mathcal{A}, \mathcal{K}, \mathcal{S}, \mathcal{V})$ where $\mathcal{Z} \subseteq \mathcal{P}$.

If A wants to sign a message x which is a bitstring of arbitrary length. She constructs the message digest $z = h(x)$ and calculates the signature on z, $y = sig_K(z)$. She then transmits the ordered pair (x, y) over the channel.

3.3.5   *ElGamal Signature Scheme*

The ElGamal Signature Scheme is a signature scheme such that there are many valid signatures for any given message and the verification algorithm accepts any of these valid signatures as genuine.

Let p be a prime such that the discrete logarithm problem in $\mathbb{Z}/p\mathbb{Z}$ is intractable and α be a generator of $(\mathbb{Z}/p\mathbb{Z})^*$. Set $P = (\mathbb{Z}/p\mathbb{Z})^*$,

$$\mathcal{A} = (\mathbb{Z}/p\mathbb{Z})^* \times \mathbb{Z}/(p-1)\mathbb{Z},$$

$$\mathcal{K} = \{(p, \alpha, a, \beta) | \beta \equiv \alpha^a \bmod p\}.$$

Here a is the private key whereas the values p, α, and β are the public keys. For $K = (p, \alpha, a, \beta)$ and a kept unknown random number

$k \in (\mathbb{Z}/(p-1)\mathbb{Z})^*$, define

$$sig_K(x, k) = (\gamma, \delta),$$

where

$$\gamma = \alpha^k \bmod p \text{ and } \delta = (x - a\gamma)k^{-1} \bmod (p-1).$$

For x, $\gamma \in (\mathbb{Z}/p\mathbb{Z})^*$ and $\delta \in \mathbb{Z}/(p-1)\mathbb{Z}$, set

$$ver_K(x, (\gamma, \delta)) = true \Leftrightarrow \beta^\gamma \gamma^\delta \equiv \alpha^x \bmod p.$$

We note that an ElGamal signature consists of two components, namely γ and δ; γ is obtained by raising α to a random power modulo p and does not depend on the message x that is signed, δ depends on the message x and the private key a.

We have

$$\beta^\gamma \gamma^\delta \equiv \alpha^{a\gamma} \alpha^{k\delta} \equiv \alpha^x \bmod p,$$

since $a\gamma + k\delta \equiv x \bmod (p-1)$. Conversely, if

$$\alpha^x \equiv \beta^\gamma \gamma^\delta \bmod p,$$

substituting $\gamma \equiv \alpha^k \bmod p$ and $\beta \equiv \alpha^a \bmod p$, we get

$$\alpha^x \equiv \alpha^{a\gamma + k\delta} \bmod p.$$

Since α is a primitive element of $(\mathbb{Z}/p\mathbb{Z})^*$,

$$x \equiv a\gamma + k\delta \bmod (p-1).$$

So given x, a, γ and k, we can solve for δ with

$$\delta \equiv k^{-1}(x - a\gamma) \bmod (p-1).$$

Hence $ver_K(x, (\gamma, \delta)) = true$.

Thus if the signature is set correctly, then the verification works.

A calculates a signature by the private key a and the secret random number k (used for signing one message x). The verification can be achieved using only public data.

We illustrate the ElGamal Signature Scheme with a numerical example. Let $p = 467$, then $\alpha = 2$ is a generator of $(\mathbb{Z}/467\mathbb{Z})^*$. Take

$a = 127$; we have

$$\beta = 2^{127} \equiv 132 \bmod 467$$

Suppose A wants to sign the message $x = 100$ and she selects the random value $k = 213$. Direct calculation gives $213^{-1} \bmod 466 = 431$,

$$\gamma = 2^{213} \equiv 29 \bmod 467,$$

and

$$\delta \equiv 431(100 - 127 \times 29) \equiv 51 \bmod 466.$$

Anyone can verify the validity of the signature $(29, 51)$ by checking

$$132^{29} 29^{51} \equiv 189 \bmod 467 \text{ and } 2^{100} \equiv 189 \bmod 467.$$

3.3.6   *Digital Signature Algorithm*

Let p be a 2048-bit prime such that the discrete logarithm in $\mathbb{Z}/p\mathbb{Z}$ is hard to deal with and q be a 224-bit prime that divides $p - 1$, $\alpha \in (\mathbb{Z}/p\mathbb{Z})^*$ has order dividing q. Set $\mathcal{P}$ to be the collection of bitstrings, $\mathcal{A} = (\mathbb{Z}/q\mathbb{Z})^* \times (\mathbb{Z}/q\mathbb{Z})^*$ and

$$\mathcal{K} = \{(p, q, \alpha, a, \beta) \mid \beta \equiv \alpha^a \bmod p\},$$

where $0 \le a \le q - 1$. Here, a is the private key and the values p, q, α and β are the public key. For $K = (p, q, \alpha, a, \beta)$, choose a secret random number k such that $1 \le k \le q - 1$ and define

$$sig_K(x, k) = (\gamma, \delta),$$

so that

$$\gamma \equiv (\alpha^k \bmod p) \bmod q \not\equiv 0,$$

and

$$\delta = (SHA3 - 224(x) + a\gamma)k^{-1} \bmod q \not\equiv .$$

For a bitstring x, set

$$e_1 = SHA3 - 224(x)\delta^{-1} \bmod q \text{ and } e_2 = \gamma\delta^{-1} \bmod q.$$

Then $ver_K(x, (\gamma, \delta)) = true$ if and only if $(\alpha^{e_1} \beta^{e_2} \bmod p) \bmod q = \gamma$.

Note that the definition of δ in this case is obtained by replacing x by $SHA3 - 224(x)$, the negative sign to positive, and the modulo to q instead of $p - 1$. Another point to note is that the probability of $\delta \equiv 0 \bmod q$ is approximately 2^{-224}.

We illustrate the digital signature algorithm with a numerical example. Take $p = 7879$, $q = 101$, $\alpha = 170 \in (\mathbb{Z}/7879\mathbb{Z})^*$ has order dividing 101, $a = 75$, $\beta = 4567$. Suppose A signs the message digest $SHA3 - 224(x) = 22$ and chooses the random value $k = 50$. She calculates

$$k^{-1} \bmod 101 \equiv 99, \gamma = (170^{50} \bmod 7879) \bmod 101,$$

and

$$\delta = [22 + 75(94)]99 \equiv 97 \bmod 101.$$

One can verify the signature $(94, 97)$ on the message digest 22 by going through the following computations:

$$\delta^{-1} \equiv 97^{-1} \equiv 25 \bmod 101, e_1 \equiv 22(25) \equiv 45 \bmod 101,$$

$$e_2 \equiv 94(25) \equiv 27 \bmod 101 \text{ and } (170^{45} 4567^{27} \bmod 7879) \bmod 101$$

$$\equiv 94 \bmod 101.$$

3.3.7 The Elliptic Curve DSA

The Elliptic Curve Digital Signature Algorithm is a signature scheme which can be viewed as a modification of the DSA to the setting of elliptic curves.

Let p be a large prime and ε be an elliptic curve defined over $\mathbb{Z}/p\mathbb{Z}$, A be a $\mathbb{Z}/p\mathbb{Z}$ point on ε of prime order q such that the discrete logarithm in the subgroup generated by A is infeasible. Set $\mathcal{P}$ be the collection of bitstrings, $\mathcal{A} = (\mathbb{Z}/q\mathbb{Z})^* \times (\mathbb{Z}/q\mathbb{Z})^*$ and

$$\mathcal{K} = \{(p, q, E, A, m, B) \mid B \equiv mA\},$$

where $0 \leq m \leq q - 1$. m is the private key whereas the values p, q, ε, A and B are the public key.

For $K = (p, q, \varepsilon, A, m, B)$ and a secret random number k, $1 \leq k \leq q - 1$, define

$$sig_K(x, k) = (r, s),$$

so that

$$kA = (u, v), r \equiv u \bmod q \not\equiv 0,$$

and

$$s \equiv k^{-1}(SHA3 - 224(x) + mr) \bmod q \not\equiv 0.$$

For a bitstring x and r, $s \in (\mathbb{Z}/q\mathbb{Z})^*$, set

$$w \equiv s^{-1} \bmod q, i \equiv w \times SHA3 - 224(x) \bmod q,$$

$$j = wr \bmod q, (u, v) = iA + jB.$$

Then $ver_K(x, (r, s)) = true$ if and only if $u \equiv r \bmod q$.

3.3.8 *Merkle Signature Scheme*

A signature scheme is a one-time signature scheme that is secure for only signing one message. Merkle came up with a signature scheme which can be used for a large (but fixed) number of signatures without increasing the size of the public key. This stems from the idea to create a binary tree (a.k.a. Merkle tree) by hashing combinations of various one time signature schemes such as the Lamport signature scheme or the Winternitz signature scheme.

For a fixed integer d, suppose there are 2^d examples of a one-time signature scheme with verification keys which we denote by $K_1, \ldots, K_2 d$.

The Merkle tree is a complete binary tree T of depth d. Suppose the nodes of T are labelled as in Figure 3.1 and satisfy the following properties:

(1) For $0 \leq l \leq d$, the 2^l nodes are consecutively labelled 2^l, $2^l + 1$, $\ldots$, $2^{l+1} - 1$.
(2) For $j \neq 1$, the parent of node j is node $\lfloor j/2 \rfloor$.
(3) Assuming one or both children of node j exist, the left child of node j is node $2j$ and the right child of node j is node $2j + 1$.

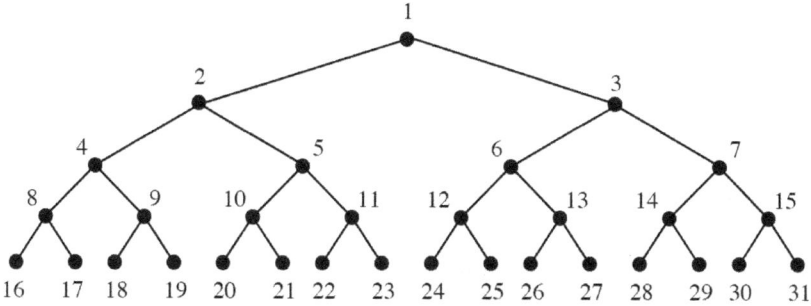

Figure 3.1: The Merkle tree.

(4) For j even, the sibling of node j is node $j + 1$. For j odd and $j \neq 1$, the sibling of node j is node $j - 1$.

Let h be a secure hash function. To each node j in T, we assign a value $V(j)$ where

$$V(j) = \begin{cases} h(V(2j)\|V(2j+1)) \, if \, 1 \leq j \leq 2^d - 1 \\ h(K_{j-2^d+1}) \, if \, 2^d \leq j \leq 2^{d+1} - 1. \end{cases}$$

The values saved in the 2^d leaf nodes are derived by hashing the 2^d public keys whereas the value saved in a nonleaf node is computed by hashing the concatenation of the values saved in its two children. $V(1)$ is the public key K for the scheme.

The ith private key is used to construct a signature m_i for the ith message which may be verified with the public key K_i, which is also part of the signature. The public key is authenticated using the Merkle tree T by giving enough data to the verifier so that he can recalculate the value of $V(1)$ and compare it with the stored value K. The required information is made up of $V(i + 2^d - 1)$ together with the values of the siblings of all the nodes in the path in T from node $i + 2^d - 1$ to node 1.

We illustrate the signature scheme with a numerical example. Assume $d = 4$ and we want to make a signature for message m_{11}. The path connecting the nodes 26, 13, 6, 3, and 1 is the relevant path and the siblings of the nodes on this path are nodes 27, 12, 7, and 2 so that $V(27)$, $V(12)$, $V(7)$, and $V(2)$ are taken as part of the signature. The key can then be authenticated by the following calculations:

(1) Calculate $V(26) = h(K_{11})$
(2) Calculate $V(13) = h(V(26)||V(27))$
(3) Calculate $V(6) = h(V(12)||V(13))$
(4) Calculate $V(3) = h(V(6)||V(7))$
(5) Calculate $V(1) = h(V(2)||V(3))$
(6) Check that $V(1) = K$.

3.3.8.1 *Digital signatures with blockchain*

Digital signatures are similar to normal signatures and depend on public-key encryption. It allows users to prove that the relevant data is authentic and retains its integrity. To create a digital signature, one inputs data through a hashing algorithm to form a unique string of numbers, and these numbers are digitally signed using the Elliptic Curve Digital Signature Algorithm (a.k.a. ECDSA algorithm) and his or her own private key. The hash and the user's private key are combined using a complex mathematical formula to produce the digital signature which can be checked with the user's public key to show that he or she is the genuine owner of the matching private key.

After the user creates his digital signature, he or she can then send it to the recipient together with the data. When the recipient receives the data, he can check its authenticity and verify whether it retains its integrity and see whether it is non-repudiable using the user's public key.

Most likely the user have shared his or her public key with the recipient, otherwise the recipient should find it on a key server. The recipient with the digital signature and the user's public key performs the reverse of the algorithm the user used. Because of the unique mathematical properties of the calculation, the result is the same as the hash of the user's data before the user digitally signed it with his or her private key.

The recipient runs the massage he received through the same hash function that the user used. If the message has not been changed after the user signed it, the hash function will return the same result from the calculation with the user's public key. If the values obtained by the user and the recipient are different, then the data has been changed or it was not signed by the user's private key or there was some other issue.

For Bitcoin and other blockchains, digital signatures are mainly used to prove ownership without revealing the private key in the transaction process.

3.4 Blockchain Mining

On any decentralized, pseudonymous network, how can we prevent people cheating to enrich themselves? Bitcoin and other blockchains resolve this issue by a peer-based verification procedure called mining.

The blockchain mining procedure can be best described by specifying that whenever a transaction is made, a copy of the contract is sent to everyone within the friendship group. After a few transactions have been completed, each person will merge the transaction details into one folder. Everybody in the friendship group would then take the result from the previous folder of transactions, combine it with current transaction details, and then try to solve a complex mathematical problems using these inputs.

The first person to find the solution will then announce it to other members of the friendship group, who will then quickly verify the correct transactions as well as the correctness of the solution.

If the answer is correct, the first person who came up with the solution receives a reward. This reward motivates everyone in the friendship group to verify the transactions. If anybody tries to cheat, the rest of the group will be alerted, and the cheaters will not be able to claim the reward so that their efforts will be wasted. Currently, the reward is set at 12.5 bitcoins.

After someone has successfully solved the mathematical problem and claimed the reward, the whole group starts collecting new transactions in another folder. When they gathered enough data, they combine these data with data from previous folder to compete and solve a new mathematical problem.

The output of the previous folder is included in the new one and a chain of output is formed. This enables people to verify the transactions on the chain are legitimate.

As everybody has a copy of the transaction history and the only effective way which is financially motivating is to honestly contribute to the validation process, double-spending and cheating are avoided. This whole procedure is performed by miners and it is automated.

If two separate miners solve a block simultaneously, the other miners will input the data from whichever block they received first and include into the next block they are working on. They will also save the data from the second block.

3.4.1   *Nodes and Miners*

A node saves a copy of the blockchain whereas a miner creates and verify the blocks. Nodes also distribute data to both users and miners and check the blocks that miners generate by ensuring the hashes match the transaction data.

3.4.2   *Timestamp*

In the Bitcoin blockchain setup, blocks of transaction data are hashed and the hash is distributed throughout the network. The hash plays the role of a timestamp, showing that the data existed when the hash was created.

Each new timestamp is one that combines the current block transaction data and the timestamp of the previous block. This creates a chain of timestamps with subsequent ones reinforcing those timestamps that precedes them.

3.4.3   *Proof-of-Work*

The Bitcoin system uses Proof-of-Work to verify its transactions. It is based on Adam Back's Hashcash scheme.

If a miner creates a block that does not match the output of the rest of the network, the block is left behind and the spent resources will be wasted. Except for exceptional situations, it is more beneficial for a miner to act honestly instead of disrupting the network or posting fake results.

This Proof-of-Work system maintains the honesty of the network. If somebody wants to change a block, he or she will have to completely do the work of solving the block again.

This Proof-of-Work system is based on the SHA-256 algorithm. This algorithm is appropriate because it is quite hard to calculate the solution but easy to verify it.

3.4.4 *Proof-of-Stake*

Proof-of-Work systems need a lot more processing power and this makes them costly in terms of infrastructure and energy. Lighter alternatives such as Proof-of-Stake are more efficient in the verification process.

There are various techniques behind Proof-of-Stake blockchain systems but they generally involve choosing the creator of the next block based on a combination of factors such as randomness, coin age, or wealth. The amount of coins a user has or the length of time the coins have been held is a measure of commitment of the user to the overall health of the system. These factors are considered together with randomness in order to prevent the blockchain from being controlled by the richest or oldest users.

Choosing the next block by Proof-of-Stake ensures that transactions are verified correctly and much more efficiently than Proof of Work systems.

3.5 Conclusion

Thus cryptography is fundamental to the inner-workings of blockchain technology. Different blockchains have different structures and apply cryptographic concepts such as public-key cryptography, digital signatures, and hashing in their own ways. These different protocols have their own unique benefits and this makes blockchains widely applicable.

References

T. ElGamal (1985). A Public-Key Cryptosystem and a Signature Scheme Based on Discrete Logarithms. *IEEE Transactions on Information Theory*, 31(4), 469–472. doi:10.1109/TIT.1985.1057074.

J. Lake (2019). Understanding Cryptography's Role in Blockchains. Comparitech. Retrieved from https://www.comparitech.com/crypto/cryptography-blockchain/ (Accessed 8 November 2019).

D. R. Stinson and M. B. Paterson (2019). Cryptography Theory and Practice. (CRC Press, Boca Raton, FL).

Chapter 4

Cryptocurrency Fork

Tan Chong Hui

Crypto-tokens and coins created as smart contracts on blockchain platforms are digital instruments that are traded and recorded by the crypto-community. This is not in virtue of having been recognized by the law or having come under the framework of financial regulation. Rather, it is the mutual recognition of the possession of a token that can be transferred from member to member and that can be exchanged with tangible goods and services within the community of users that qualify them to be financial in nature.

Seen from this perspective, the forking of crypto-tokens is very interesting indeed. Forking of financial instruments is unheard of until now. A related notion from conventional finance that one may think of is stock split. However, unlike stock splits, which produce multiple copies of the same paper, crypto-token forks can produce a replica of the entire system, which is interpreted by the users to be a distinct instrument from the original one.

Forking is not a novel concept. It is an intrinsic feature of open-source software projects. The open-source ecosystem has thrived since Linus Torvalds created Linux. One important ingredient behind the growth is the open-source licenses whose general ethos is to allow copying and to prevent hoarding. This allows software projects to be forked by developers with alternative ideas. Each fork creates a replica whose past coincides with its origin, but whose future diverges. Importantly, each fork splits up the base of contributors and users as contribution and usage of software requires time and energy.

The forking of crypto-tokens is a complicated offshoot of this basic phenomenon from the open-source space. The complication is due to the complexity of a crypto-token system, which results in the multitude of combinations of aspects of the system that can be copied over, removed, modified, or added. The client software which implements the protocol can be copied and modified. The history of interactions in the blockchain can be copied and modified. Developers and miners are divided by where they choose to contribute their time and energy. Users end up with exact copies of their crypto-tokens which begin to flow in different networks after the fork.

4.1   History of Crypto-Token Forks

One can identify three phases in the concept of forking as is generally understood by the crypto-communities. We will explain using the trendsetter Bitcoin.

In the early years of the history of Bitcoin, a fork as it was commonly discussed in the community was understood to be a divergence in the history of the transactions as it is recorded by the blockchain. The prime causes discussed were the effectiveness of the Proof-of-Work algorithm, software bugs, and sabotages by hackers. The result of such a fork is that nodes in the system end up having different views of the past that do not eventually close up and converge, becoming detrimental to the integrity of the network and hence threatening its very existence.

Starting from 2014 up till 2017, the Bitcoin community witnessed three significant forks — Bitcoin XT, Bitcoin Unlimited, and Bitcoin Classic. These embroiled the community in heated discussions over the existing protocol and what is the best way forward. To be more exact, XT, Unlimited, and Classic represent tussles over the limit of 1MB that each block is constrained to. During this phase, there appeared to be a communal effort to keep itself intact.

Suggestions to fork were restrained insofar as the underlying ideas had their pros and cons thoroughly dissected. Votes were solicited for the intended forks, which meant new software had to be installed by the users. Though the forks were launched, they had not been successful.[1] Note that many forks of the Bitcoin software have occurred over the years in the background.[2] These forks may be regarded as the vanilla forks of open-source software projects that do not carry the history of transactions and are therefore of concern to a much smaller audience. These are to be contrasted with the XT, Unlimited, and Classic forks. These latter forks had the potential to split a larger community. During this phase between 2014 and 2017, forum discussions suggest that the community needed to make a choice as a whole to move to the better option when a fork were to occur.

From 2017, the landscape has become very complicated. The Ethereum hard fork occurred in July 2015, creating Ethereum Classic alongside Ethereum. By February 2018, Ethereum Classic is still ranked in the top 20 crypto-tokens in terms of market capitalization, indicative of at least a fair degree of success of the fork.

There had been a great surge in popular interest in crypto-tokens in that year, which saw bitcoin's price against US$ increased over 18-fold. Prices of crypto-tokens in general rose significantly in tandem. This has a definite effect on motives behind forks. For now, a fork produces, seemingly at no cost, a replica comprising tokens that are likewise priced.

Three Bitcoin forks — Bitcoin Cash, Bitcoin Gold, and Bitcoin Diamond — were created under such circumstances, all within a span of four months (August–November 2017). Users who have been holding tokens prior to the fork end up having additional tokens in a new system and these are valued as well. Hardly anyone will complain about such a sweet deal. The ethos of a crypto-token fork in the current period is thus one that is mixed with the intention to

---

[1] See http://failedforks.com/
[2] See http://mapofcoins.com/bitcoin

improve the software project and the motive of token creation that is translatable to real-world value.

4.2   Comparison between Crypto-token Fork and Issuance of Other Financial Instruments

One may draw parallels between crypto-token forks at present and the genesis of a crypto-token or the issuance of a stock in an Initial Public Offering (IPO). All these acts represent the creation of a financial instrument that is exchangeable into hard currency. The exchangeability and the price at which exchanges occur are consequences of user interest, or market interest in the parlance of conventional finance. To generate and sustain interest for stocks, issuers need to go on road shows to market their stocks and they need to tend to the "fundamentals," i.e. to develop the company whose ownership the stock represents. In the same way, issuers of crypto-tokens try to talk about or to get others to talk about their wares in order to create excitement and to achieve recognition in the marketplace. At the same time, they need to make sure that the crypto-token network ecosystem that they are creating functions stably and delivers on promises.

We summarize and add to the prior discussion in Table 4.1, which comprises the various financial instruments and related entities that have been mentioned and the salient dimensions by which they have been compared. We have also added Initial Crypto-token Offering (ICO) and sovereign currency issuance to the comparison. We will discuss an ICO — the case of EOS.IO — later. New issuance of sovereign currency seldom occurs. It is not exceedingly rare either as it typically occurs at the end of a hyperinflation to replace the value-damaged old currency. Events surrounding the well-documented case of the German hyperinflation of 1919–1924 may be found in Taylor (2013)'s book on the German hyperinflation.

Table 4.1 does not in any way represent a settled state of affairs, given the current vibrant developments in the crypto-token industry. It does however signify the merit of the comparative method in

Table 4.1: Comparisons between crypto-token fork and issuance of other financial instruments.

Event/ Characteristic	Identity	Issuer	Subscriber	Accountability	Data Production	Information Flow	Price
Crypto-token Fork	Instrument is nominally linked to its origin. Quality of source code carries over.	A group of individuals that is likely to include developers at its core.	Existing owners of original token.	The community of the software project and the legal environment at large.	Transactions are produced by peers, collated at central servers. Prices are generated by brokers or at exchanges.	Announcement at an established crypto-token forum. Chatter on social media.	Development from the price of the original token, speculatively set prior to debut through opinions, arbitrary pricing, futures pricing, etc.
ICO	Instrument is implemented as a smart contract on some crypto-token platform.	Creator of the contract which is generally a group of individuals. Developers may or may not be at the core since the level of difficulty in creating the instrument is drastically reduced as compared to the case of a fork or a write-from-scratch.	Financial market participants with some degree of comfort in the posterity of virtual tokens.	The keepers of the underlying crypto-token platform and the legal environment at large.	Transactions are recorded on the blockchain having been verified by miners or stakeholders who are supposed to be blind to the nature of these transactions. Prices are generated by brokers or at exchanges.	White Paper description of the plans and prospects for coin undergird information flow between price signals and expectations in a possibly complex issuance process.	Issuance and price formation can be more complex than in an IPO, such as the case of EOS which runs on the Ethereum platform.

(Continued)

Table 4.1: (*Continued*)

Event/ Characteristic	Identity	Issuer	Subscriber	Accountability	Data Production	Information Flow	Price
Crypto-token from Scratch	For bitcoin — a novel virtual currency until it gets used in the real economy. For others — similar to bitcoin.	A group of individuals that is likely to include developers at its core.	User community that needs to be grown.	The community of the software project and the legal environment at large.	Transactions are produced by peers, collated at central servers. Prices are generated by brokers or at exchanges.	Announcement at an established crypto-token forum. Chatter on social media.	For Bitcoin — an initial struggle at price formation. Other crypto-tokens may face varying degrees of ease or difficulty in creating a market.
Stock Split	Identical to the original, only being expressed in a different denomination.	The underlying company.	Owners of the existing shares.	The public. Oversight by financial regulators.	Internal share transfers are recorded and announced. Transactions at stock exchanges are recorded in order books.	Information generally flows from private to public, going through directors, shareholders, then to the public.	Traders mentally calculate the derived price on a pro-rata basis since the change is purely denominational.

IPO	Functions just like any other stock. In addition, represents the potential of the underlying enterprise.	The underlying company.	Participants in the financial market.	The public. Oversight by financial regulators.	No financial data is available prior to the IPO. Information about the business and its potential would have been in the news or circulated among special-interest groups.	Information generally flows from private to public, going through directors, underwriters, then to the public.	Price (and number) of shares set by under-writers who bear the risk of loss due to bad estimation.
Sovereign Currency Issuance	Associated to the nation. If it is a remedy for hyperinflation, disassociation from the old currency.	The sovereign.	The citizens.	High-level ideas such as accountability, power and stability for the sovereign.	Reported by the economics ministry or produced by banks and brokers in international trade and exchange.	The sovereign exercises its influence on banks in its banking system to regulate the currency flow.	Set through top level discussions within the sovereign and with interna-tional trade partners.

finding out regularities and focal points in the investigation of a complex phenomenon.[3]

4.3   Analysis on the Bitcoin Cash Fork

We use the event analysis method to analyze the effects of forks in the crypto-token markets. Event analysis is a research technique that can be used to describe and explain interactions in complex situations and contexts. It has been employed in the fields of economics and finance as well as in anthropology and sociology where it is often required to manage and balance multiple perspectives concerning an event or events while taking into account appropriate theoretical or environmental background contexts. It can flexibly range from being qualitative to quantitative or statistical. The common denominator consists of the making sense of situations as they unfold in time or in a sequence of snapshots.

Since the objective of this research is to explicate crypto-token forks and to put them into the context of general issuance and action mechanisms of financial instruments, event analysis is a particularly suited methodology as it weaves together the key underlying aspects and factors in a natural temporal fashion. It allows us to make careful generalizations in an informed manner.

We distinguish the following three stages that characterize a crypto-token forking event:

(1) Pre-announcement stage
(2) Changes over the fork event
(3) Relatively steady state after forking

We will now apply this structure to the analysis of the Bitcoin Cash hard fork of August 2017.

---

[3]A point on terminology to note: Due to the complications alluded to earlier, many kinds of forks exist. Taxonomies exist (e.g., see https://github.com/bitc oin/bips/blob/master/bip-0099.mediawiki), but perhaps the ground is changing much faster than anyone can make a stable compilation of settled facts. The forks that we are primarily concerned with in this chapter are those that produce new financial instruments. Roughly speaking, hard forks mentioned in online literature correspond to these.

4.3.1 *Pre-Announcement Stage*

Bitcoin hard forks must be understood against the background of community debate and disagreement over the bandwidth problem in the processing of transactions. As usage of the network increases, the rate and capacity to handle transactions ought to increase in tandem. However, there is a 1MB size limit to each block that is verified by the miners. Coupling that with the dynamic difficulty adjustment which keeps the block rate at an average of 1 per 10-minutes means that the processing rate is capped by the protocol.

The decision for the 1MB size limit was made by Satoshi Nakamoto in order to protect against Denial-of-Service (DoS) attacks by hackers.[4] Unbeknownst to him then, this technical decision became a focal point of policy contention as the Bitcoin community grew.

Several proposals were made to overcome the bandwidth problem. These consist of combinations of options to modify the 1MB limit, or change the data structure while keeping the limit (SegWit), and whether to achieve the change through a soft or hard fork. Several ideas dominate and each has drawn its sub-community of supporters as well as detractors.

The Bitcoin Cash hard fork arose from a complicated political struggle within the Bitcoin community to solve the bandwidth problem. In response to the core development teams' intended implementation of BIP 148 UASF, which is meant to activate SegWit in all nodes, the Chinese miner and ASIC chip designer Bitmain announced its alternative plan for a hard fork on its corporate blog dated June 14, 2017.[5] Three teams of developers were alluded to be working on the implementation of the protocol. The first implementation of the Bitcoin Cash protocol was announced by the lead developer Amaury "Deadal Nix" Séchet of the Bitcoin ABC project at the *Future of Bitcoin* conference at Arnhem, the

---

[4]See https://www.reddit.com/r/Bitcoin/comments/3giend/citation_needed_sato shis_reason_for_blocksize/ctygzmi/?st=jd9j17hn&sh=0753e68c
[5]See https://blog.bitmain.com/en/uahf-contingency-plan-uasf-bip148/

Netherlands, held on June 30 and July 1, 2017.[6] When the dust has settled,[7] Bitcoin was forked into Bitcoin Cash on August 1, 2018, and the developer team structure behind the new protocol, like the peer-to-peer network itself, turns out to be decentralized. This is apparently a new development on the scene of crypto-token software development.

4.3.2   *Changes over the Fork Event*

An announcement to fork Bitcoin into Bitcoin Cash was made at the Bitcoin forum site bitcointalk.org,[8] dated July 22, 2017. This started a chain of forum posts on Bitcoin Cash, which is probably one of the focal point of activities on the Internet for discussions on the fork.

The fork occurred on August 1, 2017, at block height 4,78,559 (i.e., at this height, Bitcoin Cash starts to differ from Bitcoin). The last block that the Bitcoin and Bitcoin Cash networks share is thus the block at height 4,78,558 (timestamped at 2017-08-01 13:16:14).[9]

The fork is clearly visible from Figure 4.1(a), which plots the time in hours from the last common block in the two chains (height 4,78,558). While the Bitcoin block time varies roughly linearly with height in accordance to the well-known average of 10-minute per block, the block times of Bitcoin Cash display a subtle non-linearity. After an initial period during which the Bitcoin Cash block time lags behind the corresponding Bitcoin block time for the same height (the first block at height 4,78,559 to appear on the Bitcoin Cash network that is distinct from Bitcoin was timestamped at 2017-08-01 18:12:41 as compared to Bitcoin's 2017-08-01 13:23:00), the speed at which blocks are produced increased significantly. By the height 5,00,000 at

---

[6] See https://bitcoinmagazine.com/articles/future-bitcoin-cash-interview-bitcoin -abc-lead-developer-amaury-s%C3%A9chet/

[7] See https://www.bitcoincash.org/

[8] It may be found at this link: https://bitcointalk.org/index.php?topic$=$20402 21.0

[9] Blockchain data for the following analysis was collected from blockchair.com. Price data was collected from Bitfinex via the site m.investing.com. The data spans the height 4,55,000 (dated 2017-02-27 16:55:48) to the height of 5,00,000 (dated 2017-12-18 18:35:25).

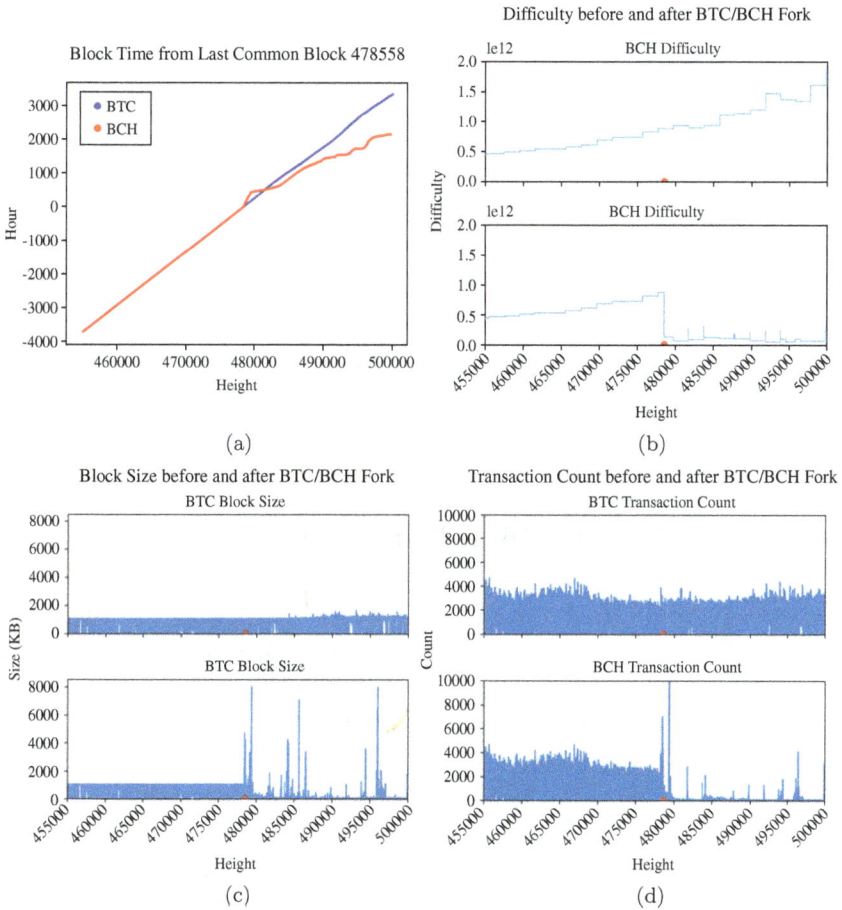

(a)

(b)

(c)

(d)

Figure 4.1: BTC/BCH Forking Statistics.

which the datasets end, Bitcoin Cash is timestamped at 2017-10-30 06:06:24 against Bitcoin's timestamp of 2017-12-18 18:35:25.

The charts in Figure 4.1(b) show the difficulty parameter for both networks. The dot on the axes marks the height at which the fork begins. Recall that difficulty is a numerical parameter that adjusts how difficult it is to verify a block, which in actuality means how fast it is on average to find a hash below a corresponding target. The Bitcoin protocol specifies that that the difficulty is recalculated every 2,016 blocks. This allows the network to maintain the block time to the average of 10-minute per block as it adjusts to the overall hashing situation of the miners. The chart for Bitcoin shows a steadily rising picture for the difficulty. This is positively correlated to the longer-term picture that the hashing power invested into the Bitcoin network has been steadily increasing over the years. It is also positively correlated to the drastically risen BTC against US$ in 2017 going on toward 2018. The chart for Bitcoin Cash shows a suddenly reduced difficulty upon forking. This is indicative of the much lower amount of hashing that is invested into the network. Also in contrast is the fact that there is no apparent drop in difficulty in the Bitcoin network after forking. Either the hashing power that is drawn away from it is negligible or new sources of computational power have been utilized on the Bitcoin Cash network.

Figure 4.1(c) shows how the size of each block varies in time for both networks. The Bitcoin network shows a roughly uniform distribution of about 1MB, indicating that the full protocol limit of 1MB per block is utilized. On the other hand, the Bitcoin Cash network exhibits block size fluctuations of up to 8MB, which is the default block size limit set in the client software. It is interesting to note that apart from the spikes in block sizes, the mean block size is actually much smaller than the 1MB average for Bitcoin. As a matter of fact, the mean block sizes for Bitcoin and Bitcoin Cash between the heights of 4,78,559 and 5,00,000 are, respectively, 953kB and 48kB.

Figure 4.1(d) shows another view of the same aspect, namely the distribution of the number of transactions in each block over time. The mean transaction numbers over the heights 4,78,559 to 5,00,000 are 1880 and 50, respectively, for Bitcoin and Bitcoin Cash. This works out to the average transaction sizes of 0.51kB and 0.96kB for the two networks, respectively.

As shown in Figure 4.2(a), the fee structures priced in terms of the currency of the network are similar for Bitcoin and Bitcoin Cash. Apart from a usual spike in the chart for Bitcoin Cash, the macro features of the charts are consistent with each other.

However, when priced in terms of US$, the fee structures diverge as illustrated by Figure 4.2(b). This is due to the bigger rise in BTCUSD as compared to BCHUSD over the same period, as one can observe from Figure 4.2(c). It is evident from the figure that the

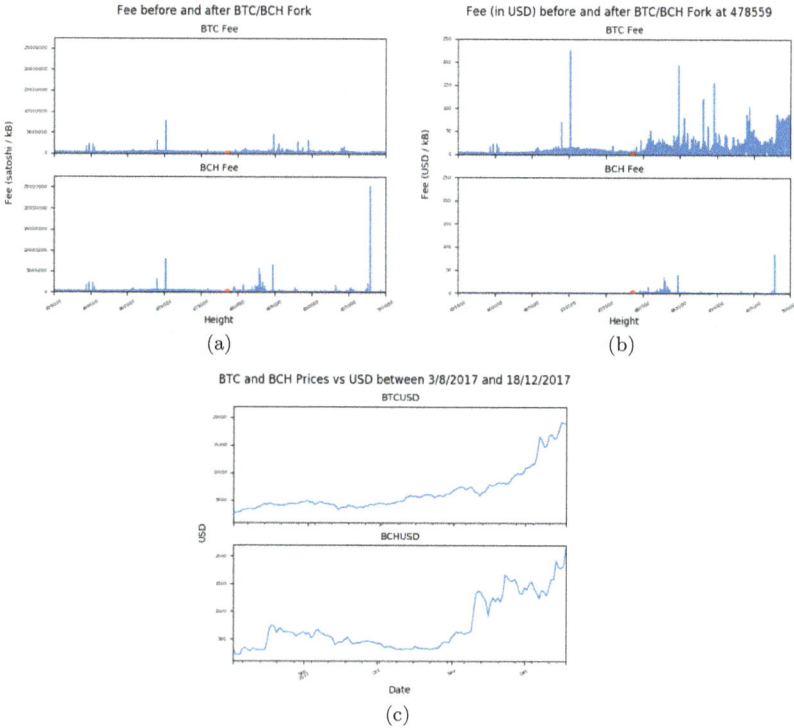

Figure 4.2: Fees and prices around the BTC/BCH Fork.

price movements of the two crypto-tokens differ by a scaling factor of 10.

The pie charts in Figure 4.3 illustrate the distribution of blocks to miners before and after the fork, as well as in the two networks after the fork.[10]

---

[10]Some explanation of the composition of the charts: The category "Others" include those miners below a certain rank as well as those miners that fall under the category "Unknown" in the raw dataset. The threshold rank is chosen simply to keep the pie charts clean and uncluttered by too many miners with small block contribution. Analyzing the raw data, we obtain that there are 14 miners who each contributes at least 2% of the total number of blocks and they collectively contribute 93% of all blocks between the heights of 4,55,000 and 4,78,558 before the fork. After the fork, between the heights of 4,78,559 and 5,00,000, there are 13 miners who each contributes at least 2% of the total number of blocks and they

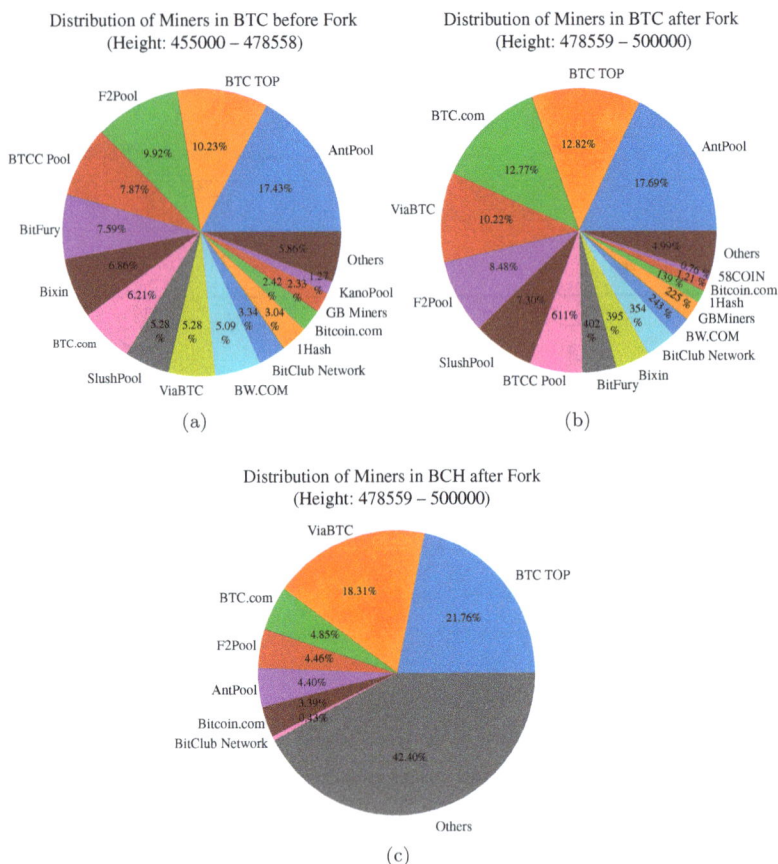

Figure 4.3: Miner distribution in BTC and BCH networks around the Fork.

4.3.3   *A Relatively Steady State after Forking*

The manifest developments leading to the fork creating Bitcoin Cash happened over a hectic short span of less than three months. The result is the first major hard fork in the history of Bitcoin.

---

collectively contribute 94% of all blocks in the Bitcoin network. The corresponding statistics for the Bitcoin Cash network are 7 miners and 99%. Only for the Bitcoin Cash case is the category "Others" at least as large as 2%. From the pie chart, "Others" in fact take up 42% here. Assuming that the category "Others" is made up of a large number of distinct small players, then one may conclude that there is a great deal of miner centralization in the Bitcoin network as compared to the Bitcoin Cash network.

In February 2018, Bitcoin Cash was ranked fourth in terms of market capitalization of all crypto-tokens. The price against US$ and the market capitalization are about eight times smaller than those of Bitcoin. This is understandable, considering the name factor. To gain further perspectives, Bitcoin Gold and Bitcoin Diamond — the two other hard forks of 2017 that occurred after Bitcoin Cash — were ranked 21 and 1,158, respectively, on February 5, 2018.[11] Ethereum Classic which was forked by Ethereum has fallen to the 17th position.

It is probably too early to tell how Bitcoin Cash will further develop.

4.4   A Comparison with ICO: The ICO of EOS.IO

In this section, we look at the ICO of EOS.IO as an example to illustrate the issuance process of crypto-token as compared to the process of a crypto-token fork.

EOS.IO is a smart contract platform that is developed by the private company Block.one. It is positioned to be a competitor of Ethereum for providing the same sort of blockchain services which roughly can be described as a decentralized app platform. It is marketed to be able to process transactions at faster speeds than Ethereum.

The ICO of EOS.IO was well-planned and complex at the same time. The complexity of the ICO is due to the fact that it is separated into many successive sessions, the details and rationale of which we will explain in a moment. Prior to the first ICO session, its executives ran many roadshows to advertise the impending ICO to would-be investors.

The ICO was planned to begin on June 26, 2017, and to end on July 3, 2018. The announcement was made that 1 billion EOS (crypto-token of the EOS.IO platform) has been planned, 900 million of which would be released over an initial 5-day period of 200 million tokens, to be followed by 350 consecutive 23-hour sessions of 2 million tokens each. The distribution of tokens in each session

---

[11] See https://coinmarketcap.com/all/views/all/

will be made on a pro-rata basis and the price per token would be determined by market demand. Block.one retained 100 million tokens and would not trade or transfer them during the token distribution period.

The rationale behind the pro-rata basis is to allow everyone with equal opportunity to invest in the token. Spreading the ICO out over consecutive sessions is intended to allow the market with its informational feedback to correctly price the tokens (which means that the average price at which the tokens are sold is equal to the market price at the end of the exercise). The initially large issuance is to accommodate the expectedly strong demand.

The manner by which an ICO is carried out as sketched here in the case of EOS.IO stands in contrast to IPOs. Banks are usually involved as intermediary in the IPOs of companies. They are paid fees for their services and they assume the risk of mispricing at the same time. This suggests that the complexity of the operations is generally pared. On the other hand, an ICO largely involves the deployment of appropriate code. This is naturally planned in-house and does not required the intervention of third parties. In this way, one may rationalize the complex ICO of EOS.IO.

4.5   Summary and Discussion

The purpose of an event analysis is to make sense, either quantitatively or qualitatively, of a sequence of situations as it rolls out in reality. The understanding that we attempt to achieve takes into account the temporal order and the necessarily integrated nature of various aspects of the phenomenon as they reveal themselves. Ultimately, the goal is for us to generalize from the particular event and locate persistent features in the context of events in which financial instruments are forked or split.

Let us therefore pose the following general-type questions that we will attempt to answer given the analysis of the Bitcoin/Bitcoin Cash fork that we have just done:

- To whom is/are the action initiators answerable?
- What are the features that characterize the fork?

- How does information flow from being private to being public?
- How do prices and other indicators change over the period of the event?
- How do the concerned people react over the event?

Arguments over the course that the Bitcoin network should take have been going on for years. On one level, these arguments are political tussles within the community between factions of users of the software that have arisen over time. To put it simply, these are the miners, developers, and the rest of the users. On another level, these arguments are exchanges over how the protocols as implemented in the client software should be shaped in the future.

The Bitcoin Cash fork arose from several forks that have been discussed in the community for the past several years. These forks, unlike the usual open-source software forks, are ones that do split the history of transactions and hence have the potential to determine the course that the ledger of possessions will take thereafter. Unlike earlier forks that did not quite succeed (Bitcoin XT, Bitcoin Unlimited, and Bitcoin Classic), the Bitcoin Cash fork was initiated by the powerful mining and ASIC chip maker Bitmain, which has been able to rally several developer groups to its proposed protocol adjustment to Bitcoin.

With developers writing the code and at least one powerful miner to verify the blocks, the only thing that was missing is a base of users. As we saw in the charts in Figure 4.1(b), the hashing power in the Bitcoin Cash network is significantly lower than that for Bitcoin. Usage as indicated by transaction count is also appreciably low. For the network to grow and to attract users, the developers will have to demonstrate its worth over its closest competitors in the crypto-token industry.

To distinguish Bitcoin Cash from Bitcoin, the developers have removed the block size 1MB limit and provided protection against replay attacks through the introduction of new transaction signature schemes. There are also several independent developer teams to provide for a decentralized software development environment.

The news about the hard fork was made public on a corporate blog of Bitmain. It was alluded that developers were implementing the proposed protocol for the hard fork. The Bitcoin ABC project which implemented the Bitcoin Cash protocol was announced shortly. Public announcement of the fork was put on the venerable Bitcoin forum bitcointalk.org. A great deal of discussions followed.

As the fork occurred at block 4,78,559 on August 1, 2017, Bitcoin Cash started to deviate from Bitcoin in its blockchain characteristics. Blocks were at first produced at a slower pace. Then the speed picked up and overtook Bitcoin's pace of 1 block per 10-minute. From the charts and calculations in Figures 4.1(c) and (d), it can be seen that the mean number of transactions and correspondingly the size of each verified block is low. However, there are several spikes that reach towards the 8MB default limit. Difficulty is significantly lower in the Bitcoin Cash network as compared to Bitcoin. The miner population also appears to be more decentralized. Price data for the first two days after the fork is not available. Presumably, that was a phase of price discovery during which erratic and irregular prices were the norm. From August 3, 2017, price data has been made available by the crypto-token Bitfinex. The trajectories show a scale difference of a factor of 10 between Bitcoin and Bitcoin Cash.

Discussions and arguments in the forums and social media are a mixed bag. There are proponents and detractors for and against each camp, both before and after the fork occurred. Some have voiced their desire to sell down the token upon forking as they did not believe in its value and see it as free money. Others talked about trading between the two crypto-tokens, presumably to capture arbitrage profits. Apart from miners, developers, and users, some prominent supporters of Bitcoin Cash also featured in the news. The overall atmosphere is one of confusing vibrancies, not unlike the conventional financial markets.

The issue of price similarity or divergence between the case of a crypto-token and its fork and the case of a conventional financial instrument is interesting and well illustrates differences in the mechanisms underlying the instruments. It is general knowledge that, in a stock split which is well-publicized prior to the event, the price adjusts on a pro-rata basis against background market movements. The price adjustment is achieved by traders who rationally calculate the new price level from which to pick up trading after the split. Each share carries with it a corresponding package of rights and claims on the issuing company so that a split represents a corresponding division of these rights and claims. The market relates the price to this essential nature of the stock and adjusts the state accordingly. In the case of government currency issuance, the power of the authority is usually sufficient to cause the market to regard a new peg or a price adjustment for the new issuance as being official. Such formal relationships are missing between a crypto-token and its fork. Hence, we witness the divergence in price between Bitcoin and Bitcoin Cash upon the fork. While no formal relationship exists, informal ones in the form of identical code base, similar ideology, and the same set of users right after the fork certainly do. This, in a qualitative sense, explains the round figure adjustment in price (1:10) in Bitcoin Cash versus Bitcoin and the highly correlated price trajectories moving forward from the split.

Reference

F. Taylor (2013). The Downfall of Money: Germany's Hyperinflation and the Destruction of the Middle Class (Bloomsbury Publishing).

Chapter 5

Application of Blockchain Technology in Private Equity

Choo Teck Li

Blockchain technology has received extensive attention in recent years due to its interesting properties (e.g., trustlessness, immutability) and "evolutionary" use cases (e.g., in trade finance, central banks, logistics). This is further amplified by the bull and bear runs of cryptocurrency, which resulted in what Gartner described as the hype cycle of blockchain technology (Litan and Leow, 2019). Large corporates have started to recognize the capabilities of blockchain technology and embarked on the journey to use blockchain technology as the next evolution of their systems. In particular, the financial market has ran forward with its experimentation by working on blockchain technology directly or indirectly (through the support for digital assets). For example, JP Morgan introduced Quorum and JPM Coin for intra-ecosystem settlement, World Bank launched blockchain-powered bonds, BNY Mellon launched its digital asset custody service, TD Ameritrade targeted to launch retail crypto-trading platform, and WeBank is running a blockchain-based digital bank servicing 400m transactions daily for 180m customers.

Private capital is also supporting the development of the industry, with Andreessen Horowitz/a16z crypto fund and Union Square Ventures being one of the more active venture capital firms in the space. Institutional money has also started to enter the crypto market in search for a low correlation product in the face of market volatility and looming recession threats. While the application of blockchain technology to private equity industry is nascent, there are already some promising results. For example, Northern Trust Corporation uses blockchain technology for its fund administration, and companies such as Prometheum and Xen are looking to tokenize private equity funds.

There is little research exploring how the capital market would be reshaped when tokenization of assets becomes mainstream. For example, would venture capital and private equity still makes sense? Would there be a need for mergers and acquisition (M&A) lawyers if there were coded governance? How would interoperability of different blockchains look like? Would valuation of tokens look like prices of public stocks? Would fungible or non-fungible tokens be the dominant form? Would the history of past ownership make the token less or more valuable? Or would hostile takeovers become easier? With all these questions in mind, it would be helpful to investigate how private equity could be impacted when asset tokenization becomes widely adopted so that the industry can prepare for such a disruption.

In this chapter, we discuss how blockchain technology can be applied to the traditional private equity industry and how the tokenization of assets would disrupt the industry and reshape the private fundraising landscape. We explore the role of private equity in this renewed world, and the relevant blockchain-related technology required (apart from the tokenization).

5.1   Introduction

5.1.1   *Fundraising*

Broadly speaking, fundraising can be segmented into two approaches — private and public. For private capital, sources can be less institutional such as friends and family, or more institutional such as corporates, venture capital, and private equity. For public capital, sources can also be less institutional such as crowdfunding, to more institutional such as listing on an exchange. The financial instrument (e.g., debt, equity) used is also a consideration as it can affect the cost of funding and influence the operations of the business.

Traditionally, startups have limited options in terms of funding — they are unable to raise money from the public due to regulations as well as not possessing the track record that attracts public monies. Startups usually have to rely on private sources such as friends and family, angel investors, and venture capital (depending on maturity of the company). It is only in recent years that through the proliferation and hype of the blockchain technology that young companies or projects found an alternative method to raise money such as via Initial Coin Offerings (ICOs), Initial Exchange Offerings (IEOs), and Security Token Offerings (STOs). While regulations can be an issue, there are several jurisdictions where these new methods of fundraising are starting to be accepted. Many countries remain unclear about their regulations on token offerings. Table 5.1 shows selected jurisdictions and the regulatory view of ICO, IEO, and STOs.

As one of the world's most advanced economies, the US has been looked at to crosscheck the utility of cryptocurrencies and tokenization. The country transited from recognizing all cryptocurrencies as securities via the Howey Test (Peirce, 2019), to clarifying that bitcoin is not a security (Rooner, 2018a), and more recently, that Ethereum is a commodity (Roberts, 2019). While the recognition is not on tokenization itself, it brings color and helps to shape the view on tokenization as a form of fundraising mechanism. The recent commitment from China to seize the opportunity for

Table 5.1: Jurisdictions and regulatory view of ICOs, IEOs, and STOs.

	Friendly	Unfriendly
ICO/IEO	Singapore, Switzerland, Gibraltar, Estonia, Thailand	US, China
STO	Singapore, Australia, Hong Kong, US	China, Vietnam, South Korea

Source: Law Library of Congress (n.d.) and Fintechnews.sg (2019).

blockchain leadership and improve on areas such as SME financing (Liu, 2019), and its development of a central bank digital currency (i.e., digitalized Chinese Yuan) (Browne, 2019) also brings hope that tokenization could be a mainstream fundraising mechanism in the future.

5.1.2 Advantages and Disadvantages of Private Equity

As an industry, private equity is favored as a source of capital as the fund managers are able to provide value-addition on top financial help. Private equity fund managers are skilled at assembling a strong and highly motivated management teams together, identifying critical strategic levers that drive performance, and selling or listing businesses at good valuations (Barber and Goold, 2007). For earlier-stage companies, private equity fund managers focusing on venture capital strategy provide credibility and legitimacy, which in turn attract more outside financing (Baeyens and Manigart, 2003).

However, private equity may not always be the best source of capital. Private equity vehicles are usually structured with a fixed lifetime — 7 years for RMB-denominated funds and 10 years for US$-denominated funds. While this may create stress and discipline for private equity fund managers to work within the timeline to create value, the urgency for a liquidity event also means that fund managers may be forced to exit prematurely, be it through trade sales, M&A, or initial public offering (IPO). Several big tech companies such as Snap, Lyft, and Uber that went IPO under the pressure to exit, saw a significant drop in their valuation/market capitalization. In addition, the cost of equity is also typically higher compared to cost of debt. Founders will also have to fight against the dilution of their stakes and the discretion on business decisions as investors are usually given board seats.

5.1.3 Advantages and Disadvantages of Tokenization

Tokenization of security is recognized to provide benefits such as fractionalization of larger assets, increased liquidity, lower issuance fees, and greater market efficiency (Koffman, 2018). Security token issuers can also access a global pool of capital and achieve better market exposure as the deals would be public and visible to anyone with internet connection (Marks, 2018). Tokenization of assets on financial markets can also increase the profitability of the security issuer through the quicker execution time and higher liquidity while having reliability not inferior to traditional products (Davydov and Khalilova, 2019).

Tokenization has barely made an entrance into the institutional world. While tokenization could potentially be used as an easier way to raise funds, it seems at this moment that it is unable to provide the same types of benefits as traditional venture capital or private equity firms. In addition, there are usually cautious regulations that limit fundraising from retail investors in order to protect them. However, that does not denounce the possibility that there could be a hybrid model of tokenization and traditional venture capital. For example, there could be scenarios where venture capital takes a significant stake in a round of tokenization or given better terms than the public for bringing that "venture capital edge" to the company. This is not impossible, given that there are already several funds in the market (e.g., Polychain Capital, a16z crypto fund, and Fenbushi Capital) that invests into tokens. We can expect that as the space becomes more mature, there will be more equity-token hybrid funds and (non-speculative) token funds. Some of these funds have already started to differentiate themselves, such as by being involved in the token design, be it in terms of legal (e.g., structuring of rights, different class of "shares"), technology (e.g., smart contracts, transparency), or token economics.

5.2 Current Developments

5.2.1 *Fund Administration*

The blockchain technology makes sense for fund administration, as it is able to bring efficiency, reduce cybersecurity risk, and remove the need for trust. General Partners (GPs; i.e., fund managers) typically issue capital call and distribution notices, as well as valuation reports to Limited Partners (LPs; i.e., financial investors). Upon receiving these capital notices and reports, LPs would verify and process them. The process includes the entering of the received data into the LPs' database system. With blockchain technology, LPs could skip the step of re-entering the data as the GP has already digitized the data when they send out the notices and reports, and LPs simply have to verify or read the ledger. There can be consensus mechanisms set up to verify the data automatically or dispute the entry off-chain should there be an error. For the former, data can be verified easily as there are usually formulae for calculating items such as management fees and carried interests. Items that are non-verifiable, such as investment amount, can be disputed off-chain and settled via new capital call or refund entries. Delegated Proof-of-Stake can be an interesting consensus protocol to use, because third-party actors can help to validate transactions and be rewarded or have their stakes "slashed" should they act maliciously.

There are currently vendors that offer services to process fund administrative work on behalf of LPs. However, the adoption rate is not high. There are generally two models — human-driven or machine-driven. For models that use humans to process, LPs would still have to verify the entries, which may be fraught with human errors. There are many operational kinks to overcome, as there is no standard format for capital notices and valuation reports. As such, the substitution of middle office personnel with dedicated vendor staff may make sense from a scale perspective, but may not reduce the rate of human errors significantly (especially for the initial phase of learning new formats). For models that use machines to process, there are limitations concerning the state of the Optical Character Recognition (OCR) technology. Most OCR techniques today use Artificial Intelligence (AI), which would require the re-training of the algorithms as well as sufficient historical data to train (which may be a challenge for new funds) when there are different formats introduced.

Both GPs and LPs are also concerned about sharing their investment data — GPs do not want to reveal their fund performance to a third party who they do not trust, while LPs do not want to voluntarily disclose the type of investments they have made.

By deploying blockchain, GPs and LPs can remove the need for a third-party vendor. Even if the presence of the vendor is preferred (e.g., for verification), the use of privacy-enforcing techniques such as zero-knowledge proofs can help to circumvent the problem of needing to share data.

Companies such as Northern Trust Corporation and Rivver have already developed beyond conceptual phase and into commercial phase. Northern Trust launched their first deployment of blockchain technology for the private equity industry in 2017 (Northern Trust, 2019). The platform enhances capital and cashflow management as well as automates the middle office functions in private equity firms. Northern Trust has since transferred the technology to Broadridge Financial Solutions, a NYSE-listed company and a spinoff of ADP, which has been providing technology support to financial services companies since 2007, to deliver an industry-wide PE blockchain solution. Rivver is another company that has moved beyond a conceptual stage to sign on several venture capital funds to handle their fund administration as well as Big Four audit companies and law firms to run their nodes. The Israeli startup was founded in 2018, and the rapid pace of its development can be taken as a sign of acceptance from the private equity market.

5.2.2 *Tokenization*

According to Deloitte (Laurent *et al.*, 2018), the tokenization of assets refers to the process of issuing a blockchain token (i.e., security token) that digitally represents a real tradable asset. This is similar to the traditional process of securitization but done through the usage of blockchain technology. The security tokens are digital representation of the security (e.g., a share in a company, ownership of real estate, or stake in an investment fund) and are distributed via STO. These security tokens are also typically tradeable in the secondary market.

Companies such as Prometheum, Xen, and 1exchange are working on tokenization platforms where securities such as real estate, hedge funds, and private equity funds can be made into tokens and traded. Some of these platforms achieve this by first having a vehicle to invest in the fund, and thereafter tokenize the vehicle. This usually involves using semi-fungible tokens and tracking the ownership of the assets and the movement of the capitalization table 24/7. For existing investors and founders, security token platforms could provide another avenue for exit as well as increased ease of liquidity (e.g., skip lengthy and expensive administrative work). For the new investors, the quality of security tokens available is dependent on the platform's sourcing capability. There is also limited room for new investors to conduct his or her due diligence as the platforms target scale.

The tokenization process is dependent on the regulation in the different jurisdictions. For example, in Singapore, tokenization platforms would require a Recognized Market Operator (RMO) license issued by the MAS to operate, and the projects would have to comply with the Securities and Futures Act (MAS, 2018). In the US, STOs are done via Regulation A+ offering under the JOBS Act (SeedInvest, 2016). BlockStack became a testament to the viability of a US token offering by becoming the first SEC-qualified token sale (De, 2019). The main concern for regulators around security token offering is the protection of retail investors. While different jurisdictions may have differing laws, the majority of regulations tend to prefer fundraising from accredited investors.

5.3   Future of Fundraising

5.3.1   *Outlook*

The future of fundraising will likely be a hybrid of the traditional private equity and tokenization. There are several ways to play this out, but we can broadly segment it into two categories: equity-based and asset-based.

For equity-based funding, this is similar to the traditional private equity play where companies trade their equity stake in the company in exchange for capital. The only thing different is the form factor where the equity is now held in tokens (i.e., security tokens) instead of share certificates. These tokens can be sold to institutional investors or retail investors, depending on the discretion of the company or the regulations in the jurisdiction. Similar to the typical investment cycle, investors can choose to hold the tokens until the day they want to liquidate or exit the position. This can be done via an organized exchange platform or private transaction. In the traditional world, a third party will be needed to intermediate the trade so that the transaction would be executed fairly. Using blockchain, this can be done on a trustless basis on-chain via mechanisms such as atomic swap.

For asset-based funding, this will be similar to offering utility coins in ICOs and the concept of leaseback in traditional finance. In this approach, the tokens that the company issues are utility tokens as they represent an access right in the network or an asset itself. The raising of fund via the sale of utility tokens is essentially a sale of asset even though the asset still has to reside within the system because it has no value otherwise. This is similar to a leaseback because the network "leases" out the token in exchange for funds. Other analogies would be arcade tokens and casino chips. The "owners" of these tokens can choose to hold for as long as they wish, and liquidate them via exchange platforms or private transaction using the likes of atomic swaps.

Just like how a company may raise capital through different means in a traditional finance setting, companies could also use both tokenization mechanisms to raise funds. For example, a company may raise via the equity method and later raise through the asset method. It may be preferable to first raise via equity then asset method to maximize the funding from the token issuance. This is because equity funding from fund managers can bring operational expertise and networks which would grow the business. The issuance of utility tokens thereafter could then be priced higher and provide a higher fundraising amount for the company as well as a higher upside for its investors.

The choice for equity fundraising would likely continue to be preferred, as professional fund managers would want to have control in the company. However, we should not belittle the influence of ICO — the top 10 ICOs to date range between US$150m and US$4b (Rooney, 2018b). Furthermore, many of these projects do not even have a live product or proven revenue stream.

Even though with blockchain technology, fundraising can be done more conveniently and safely due to decreased human interventions, it may not necessarily be significantly faster than existing solutions. This is because the company going for listing would still need to consult with the regulators multiple times in order for the regulators to get comfortable with the company and approve it to raise fund from the market. In addition, if tokenization becomes mainstream, the lower hurdles (e.g., costs) to raise funds would also result in waves of companies seeking to tokenize themselves.

Fundraising is just one phase of a company's lifecycle; there are several other events such as M&A, listing, or new rounds of capitalization as the company grows. As tokenization requires a very different infrastructure from other financial instruments used even in modern finance, there would be a need for "interoperability." For example, during M&A, how would the acquirer acquire the tokens of the target if it does not have sufficient capability to store tokens in an "institutional" way? How does the company do a traditional public listing if it has done an STO before — should the tokens still exist or be burnt and converted to a normal share certificate; or should the traditional exchange offer tokenization as well? If it is the latter, would the tokens reside on different networks or brought to the later tokenization platform's network? Things may also become more complicated if the tokens issued are not of the same standards (e.g., ERC-1400 vs SRC-20). Perhaps one way to solve this is to rely on digital custody solutions. These digital custody solution providers would have the scale to support a variety of token standards and store tokens at an enterprise-grade level. The transfer of storage risks to these custody solution providers also help to save on insurance cost.

5.3.2   *Coded Governance*

An interesting feature of blockchain technology is its ability to provide coded governance. This takes the "code is law" approach where upgrades and software changes are hardcoded into the protocol once voted in favor by the community (Mappo, 2019). On-chain governance can provide faster confirmation times and decentralized decision-making. However, the drawbacks are that it requires the participation of the voter community, which can be a challenge at scale, and assumes that all voters would act in the interest of the broader community (Mappo, 2019). In the case of private equity, having a coded governance may be difficult to begin with. For instance, there are no fixed template for legal agreements even within geography, and clauses are often left unclear due to different interpretations as they are not necessary to be disputed at the point of signing. This may result in a defunct governance or loopholes that may be exploited (such as in the DAO incident). There have been efforts such as by the International Limited Partner Association (ILPA) to set industry-wide templates (ILPA, 2019), although adoption rate has not been high. For the LPs, the existence of side letter agreements that are off-template can also make coded governance trickier.

There have been practitioners who propose that coded governance be "pushed" to the market, and parties interested would sign up while those who do not agree with the terms can simply walk away. This approach may be feasible if the deal is of high demand, but most deals in the market do not enjoy the same good fortune. Many institutional investors have their list of unique "no-no's," and the agreements have to be sufficiently flexible. The solution perhaps would be to have only the essential and indisputable parts of the agreements put on-chain (e.g., calculation of carried interest, right of first refusal). It is likely that legal opinion would still be necessary to help advice on transactions in the short- to medium-term, rather than leaving it all up to coded governance. However, it is not unforeseeable for coded governance to run an ecosystem in the further future.

5.3.3 *Valuation*

In the event that a company that has done an STO decides to list itself on a traditional exchange or a listed company decides to do an STO, would the trading price of the shares on the listed exchange be the same as the price of the tokens? The answer would likely be no. Fundamentally, the equity stake should be worth the same since it is from the same company. However, prices are subjected not only to the inherent/fundamental valuation of the product but also the economics of supply and demand. The closest point of reference would be the H-share and A-share market. The A-shares typically trade at a premium to H-shares from the same company due to a higher liquidity in the H-shares which foreign investors can trade (Investopedia, 2019). Similarly, we can expect listed shares and tokens to trade at a difference due to the type of investors available on the two platforms (due to regulatory restriction and mandate).

Some suggest that the value of the token may be less or more valuable if there is a history of ownership/transaction. For example, if the token was owned by a criminal that may have been used in illicit activities, users may want to avoid being associated with the token for fear of being embroiled in the case or have the tokens repossessed. That said, it is difficult for the users to track if previous owners have criminal records or have used it for illicit activities, and hence cannot control the token to receive anyway.

5.3.4   *Partially Fungible Tokens*

At present, fungible tokens are the standard of choice for utility tokens while the non-fungible tokens are preferred for collectibles. There is a new standard created just for the needs of security tokens. These tokens are partially fungible and created to meet the regulatory requirement of securities (e.g., KYC, AML, lock-up period, restrictions on participants) (micobo GmbH, 2018). The ERC-1400 family of tokens are the most popular standard at the moment, as it allows the token contract to partition a token holder's balances into tranches (within which are fungible; while non-fungible outside). The standard is backward compatible to the ERC-20 and ERC-777 standards to operate at the tranche and non-tranche level (Dossa, 2018).

5.3.5   *Hostile Takeovers*

In a tokenized world, hostile takeovers would likely be harder to achieve than in the traditional world. In the event that a blockchain-based company is facing an impending hostile takeover, it can choose to hard-fork itself and try to migrate its resources and stakeholders over to the new network (Bromberg, 2018). However, this can be complicated if the company is not based on blockchain. The company can delay the hostile takeover by invoking the common "poison pill" clause to dilute new ownership by issuing deeply-discounted new shares to existing shareholders triggered when a shareholder passes a specified threshold of percentage ownership. In the token setting, to incentivize token holders to stay and "fight" the hostile takeover, the original smart contract can be coded to reissue and distribute tokens pro-rata to all existing token holders when a certain percentage of tokens outstanding are burnt within a specific period of time (Bromberg, 2018).

5.4 Technologies Needed

While the technologies required for tokenization may already be offered in the market, adoption could remain low due to limited functionality or not being sufficiently enterprise-grade. The following are technologies that would likely be needed in order for mainstream adoption to happen.

5.4.1 *Interoperability*

There is a need for the different blockchains to work with each other. For example, the blockchain that the fund manager has should be able to communicate with the blockchains of their portfolio companies so that they can receive accurate information at (near) real-time, while not enforcing every party to use the same type of blockchain framework (e.g., Hyperledger, Ethereum). Several protocols are being built out now. The two most popular projects are Polkadot and Cosmos. Polkadot is creating a platform where all other blockchains can connect to, while Cosmos is more focused on the sovereignty of the chains and have hubs instead (Choi, 2019). Polkadot and Cosmos will likely face more compatibility issues (despite already building bridge chains and peg zones) as they scale up.

5.4.2 *Atomic Swaps*

While atomic swaps have been proven to work (such as through Hash-Time Locked Contracts), there are still several inefficiencies in the technology. For example, atomic swaps are not always fast, and compatibility can be an issue (Dalton, 2019). Transaction fees can also be a concern, which may make it less appealing than trading through an intermediary.

5.4.3 *Fiat-crypto On/Off-ramp*

In order for mainstream adoption to happen, it must be sufficiently easy to change from fiat to crypto and vice versa. Most people still hold fiat currency, a trend that is unlikely to reverse in the short to medium term. Other than the technology behind moving between fiat and crypto, compliance would likely be the main time-intensive component in the process.

5.4.4 *Layer 2 Technology*

There are many Layer 2 projects working to solve the scalability problem, of which state channels and side-chains are two examples of off-chain approach that have gathered interest. However, the technologies still have room for improvements — state channels still need to solve the exit problem where additional amount of time is required to lapse for state finality, while side-chains has the chicken-and-egg issue on the degree of the verification (e.g., is 50%–66% too much or too little) of the side chains when it exits to the main chain (Skidanov, 2019).

5.4.5 *Custody/Storage*

There will be a need for institutional-grade custody solutions if institutional investors are to work with tokens. There is currently no one storage method that allows security and accessibility — hot storage is susceptible to digital theft and cold storage is inconvenient and cumbersome (e.g., storing assets in separate private keys/wallets which are printed into sheets of paper protected by a safe box that resides in a Faraday's cage). The QuadrigaCX incident has also caused many to be cautious of being overly reliant on one person to keep safe of the private keys.

5.4.6 *Oracles*

Tokenization would benefit from oracles as it can bring on data from the real world to the blockchain. This is useful in scenarios such as when collecting data from the Internet that may affect the valuation of the portfolio company/security token. However, oracles can be influenced to forward erroneous information into the blockchain as it is difficult to make it sufficiently decentralized (Fecke, 2018).

5.5 Future Developments

Tokenization currently focuses on digitizing equity stakes on the blockchain. As equity stakes are essentially representation of rights, there is more that can be done than just proving ownership. For example, equity tokens can act as an identity proof. Currently, there are no direct links between proof of ownership (i.e., share certificate) and the access to a company's information (e.g., financial report). Tokens representing equity stakes can serve as keys to provide direct access to financial reports and other investor-only information about the company. The same token can also allow ease of voting during annual general meetings, without having to provide traditional identity documents that are not as conveniently stored as a token in the mobile phone. On the company's end, the blockchain can be split into different access restriction levels and award authority to access accordingly.

Going one step further, tokens can even become a tool to promote alignment and loyalty. At present, owning a stake in a company is purely financial and independent from one's lifestyle. There may be benefits in having the ownership token to advance certain advantages of being a shareholder to promote alignment and continued interest in the company. For example, the shareholders of a tech company can enjoy special rates when buying the company's products. This is similar to the concept of staff discounts, where the intention is to align the staff with the company and at the same time increase revenue and marketing impact. In such a world, the concept of ownership and membership blurs. For the public market, this may help to reduce volatility and fear-driven dumping of shares by retail investors who do not have an attachment with the companies they invest into and sees them solely as a tool for financial gains.

This fresh concept for fundraising can greatly benefit startups or new projects who need support in their early stages. This is also similar to how crowdfunding platforms such as Kickstarter and Indiegogo, where new projects raise capital through a promise for "sample" products or services in the future. Shareholders becomes involved in the growing journey of the startup (such as being a consumer themselves), and be more motivated to help the company succeed instead of just being financial supporters. This is possible because of the lower ticket sizes required and thus lower barrier to entry for involvement, through tokenization.

In the core IT system for private equity firms, other than fund administration, blockchain can also enable the portfolio management function. For the GPs, they could negotiate for their portfolio companies to put their data on the blockchain where the GPs can access. These data may be in the form of company quarterly reports verified by auditors and placed on the blockchain (be it the portfolio companies' or the auditors' network). This would reduce the effort and time needed to communicate data between the GPs and their portfolio companies.

For the LPs, the verified data collected from the fund administration process can be updated into the system — the quarterly and annual report for the valuations, and the capital call and distribution notices for the period in-between reports. With sufficient historical data, LPs can better predict the rate of their drawdown and triangulate with their deployment run rate to manage their investment commitments and cash flow better. To improve their management of existing portfolio, LPs can have a system to collect information available in the internet of their portfolio companies and underlying portfolio companies (i.e., portfolio companies invested by the GPs) such as via oracles. Information collected can include new fundraising rounds that the GPs did not participate in, and negative news reported of the invested companies. This is especially helpful given that LPs usually have too many underlying portfolio companies to monitor and rely too much on the GPs who do not always report sufficiently on the portfolio companies beyond the mandatory valuation figures.

With data hygiene, AI can be used by both GPs and LPs to better predict when the next fundraising round is going to happen for the companies of interest. This would give extra and meaningful time for investors to engage with and understand the target company better. This gives mindshare for the investors to secure allocation when the fundraising begins.

5.6 Conclusion

Tokenization will open up the concentrated investment world to the mass, and companies will see their investor base to be a lot more diverse. However, traditional private equity firms would still likely be a going concern given the skillsets they have to help a company grow or undergo a turnaround. These skillsets are niche and not easily replicated. That said, with the increased adoption of blockchain technology and tokenization, private equity firms would have to adapt to the new forms of fundraising and the competition it may bring. The industry has to be clearer on its role, focus on its unique advantages, and continue to add value so that it can remain relevant in an increasingly transparent world where financial prowess and information asymmetry begin to matter less.

References

Allied Market Research (2018). Personal Finance Software Market by Product Type (Web-based Software and Mobile based Software) and End User (Small Businesses Users and Individual Consumers) — Global Opportunity Analysis and Industry Forecast, 2017-2023.

K. Baeyens and S. Manigart (2003). The Role of Venture Capital. *The Journal of Private Equity Winter*, 50–58.

F. Barber and M. Goold (2007). The Strategic Secret of Private Equity. *Harvard Business Review*. Retrieved from https://hbr.org/2007/09/the-strategic-sec ret-of-private-equity (Accessed 15 January 2021).

A. Bromberg (2018). What the First Token Hostile Takeover Could Look Like. *Medium*, March 16. Retrieved from https://medium.com/@andy_bromberg /what-the-first-token-hostile-takeover-could-look-like-c40be3ccb6b5 (Acce ssed 15 January 2021).

R. Browne (2019). China's Central Bank Says It's Close to Releasing Its Own Digital Currency. *CNBC*, August 12. Retrieved from https://www.cnbc.

com/2019/08/12/china-central-bank-close-to-releasing-digital-currency-pboc-official.html (Accessed 15 January 2021).

J. Choi (2019). Demystifying Cosmos: Atomic Swaps, Ethereum, Polkadot and the Path to Blockchain Interoperability. *Medium*, March 31. Retrieved from https ://medium.com/the-spartan-group/demystifying-cosmos-atomic-swaps-eth ereum-polkadot-and-the-path-to-blockchain-interoperability-d1a2d75c20d6 (Accessed 15 January 2021).

M. Dalton (2019). Can Atomic Swaps Reach Critical Mass? *Cryptobriefing*, September 24. Retrieved from https://cryptobriefing.com/atomic-swaps-rea ch-critical-mass/ (Accessed 15 January 2021).

V. Davydov and M. Khalilova (2019). Business Model of Creating Digital Platform for Tokenization of Assets on Financial Markets. Retrieved from https://iopscience.iop.org/article/10.1088/1757-899X/497/1/012069/p df (Accessed 15 January 2021).

N. De (2019). Blockstack's Regulated Token Offerings Raise $23 Million. Coin-desk, September 10. Retrieved from https://www.coindesk.com/blockstacks -regulated-token-offerings-raise-23-million (Accessed 15 January 2021).

A. Dossa (2018). What Do In-Game Credits, Plasma Cash and Secu-rity Tokens Have in Common? Polymath, September 21. Retrieved from https://blog.polymath.network/what-do-in-game-credits-plasma-cash -and-security-tokens-have-in-common-1b490843ab85 (Accessed 15 January 2021).

M. Fecke (2018). The Problem of Blockchain Oracles — Interview with Alexander Egberts. *Legal Tech Blog*, March 27. Retrieved from https://legal-tech-blog. de/the-problem-of-blockchain-oracles-interview-with-alexander-egberts (Accessed 15 January 2021).

Fintechnews.sg (2019). STO & ICO Regulations in Asia: 2019 Edition, March 27. Retrieved from https://fintechnews.sg/29763/blockchain/ico-sto-regulation -asia-2019/ (Accessed 15 January 2021).

ILPA (2019). ILPA Publishes Model Limited Partnership Agreement to Strengthen LP-GP Alignment in the Private Equity Industry. *Globewire*, October 30. Retrieved from https://www.globenewswire.com/ news-release/2019/10/30/1937739/0/en/ILPA-Publishes-Model-Limited-Pa rtnership-Agreement-to-Strengthen-LP-GP-Alignment-in-the-Private-Equi ty-Industry.html (Accessed 15 January 2021).

Investopedia (2019). H-Shares. May 7. Retrieved from https://www.investopedi a.com/terms/h/hshares.asp (Accessed 15 January 2021).

T. Koffman (2018). Your Official Guide to the Security Token Ecosystem. *Medium*, April 14 Retrieved from https://medium.com/@tatianakoffman/y our-official-guide-to-the-security-token-ecosystem-61a805673db7 (Accessed 15 January 2021).

P. Laurent, T. Chollet, M. Burke and T. Seers (2018). The Tokenization of Assets is Disrupting the Financial Industry. Are You Ready? *Deloitte*, November. Retrieved from https://www2.deloitte.com/content/dam/Deloitte/lu/Docu ments/financial-services/lu-tokenization-of-assets-disrupting-financial-indu stry.pdf (Accessed 15 January 2021).

Law Library of Congress (n.d.). Regulation of Cryptocurrency Around the World. Retrieved from https://www.loc.gov/law/help/cryptocurrency/world-surve y.php (Accessed 15 January 2021).

A. Litan and A. Leow (2019). Hype Cycle for Blockchain Technologies. *Gartner*, July 11. Retrieved from https://www.gartner.com/en/documents/3947355/ hype-cycle-for-blockchain-technologies-2019 (Accessed 15 January 2021).

Z. Liu (2019). Chinese President Xi Jinping Calls for More Research, Investment Into Blockchain Technology. *South China Morning Post*, October 26. Retrieved from https://www.scmp.com/news/china/diplomacy/article/303 4716/chinese-president-xi-jinping-calls-more-research-investment (Accessed 15 January 2021).

Mappo (2019). Blockchain Governance 101. Medium, February 8. Retrieved from https://medium.com/aelfblockchain/blockchain-governance-101-bd4d d978c7c6 (Accessed 15 January 2021).

H. Marks (2018). The Future of US Securities Will Be Tokenized. *Hackernoon*, May 15. Retrieved from https://hackernoon.com/the-future-of-us-securities -will-be-tokenized-c469d41d81a1 (Accessed 15 January 2021).

MAS (2018). A Guide to Digital Token Offerings. November 30. Retrieved from ht tps://www.mas.gov.sg/\$\sim\$/media/MAS/News%20and%20Publications/ Monographs%20and%20Information%20Papers/Guide%20to%20Digital%20 Token%20Offerings%20last%20updated%20on%2030%20Nov.pdf (Accessed 15 January 2021).

micobo GmbH (2018). Security Tokens — An ERC-Standards Comparison. *Medium*, December 13. Retrieved from https://medium.com/@micobo/secur ity-tokens-an-erc-standards-comparison-919e7c379f37 (Accessed 15 January 2021).

Northern Trust (2019). Northern Trust to Transfer Pioneering Private Equity Blockchain Technology Platform to Broadridge, June 26. Retrieved from https://www.northerntrust.com/asia-pac/pr/2019/northern-trust-to-transfer-pe-blockchain-technology-to-broadridge (Accessed 15 January 2021).

H. M. Peirce, (2019). How We Howey. U.S. Securities and Exchange Commission, May 9. Retrieved from https://www.sec.gov/news/speech/peirce-how-we-h owey-050919 (Accessed 15 January 2021).

D. Roberts (2019). CFTC Says Cryptocurrency Ether is a Commodity, and Ether Futures Are Next. *Yahoo Finance*. October 10. Retrieved from https://finance.yahoo.com/news/cftc-says-cryptocurrency-ether-is-a -commodity-and-is-open-to-ether-derivatives-133455545.html (Accessed 15 January 2021).

K. Rooney (2018a). SEC Chief Says Agency Won't Change Securities Laws To Cater To Cryptocurrencies. *CNBC*, June 11. Retrieved from https://www.cnbc.com/amp/2018/06/06/sec-chairman-clayton-says-agency-wont-change-definition-of-a-security.html? (Accessed 15 January 2021).

K. Rooney (2018b). A Blockchain Start-up Just Raised $4 billion Without a Live Product. *CNBC*, May 31. Retrieved from https://www.cnbc.com/2018/05/31/a-blockchain-start-up-just-raised-4-billion-without-a-live-product.html (Accessed 15 January 2021).

SeedInvest (2016). Raising Capital using a Regulation A+ Mini-IPO. SeedInvest. October 28. Retrieved from https://www.seedinvest.com/blog/jobs-act/raising-capital-reg-a-mini-ipo (Accessed 15 January 2021).

A. Skidanov (2019). Overview of Layer 2 approaches: Plasma, State Channels, Side Chains, Roll Ups. NearProtocol, June 20. Retrieved from https://nearprotocol.com/blog/layer-2/ (Accessed 15 January 2021).

Chapter 6

Digital Payments

Liu Wenting

Global digital payment sustained double-digit growth with the cautions of the underlying trend toward industry disruption and the imperative for near-term transformation in order to maintain a dynamic industry that continues to break new ground.

McKinsey Global Payments Report 2018

The digital payments industry has sustained a remarkable growth in recent years. Global digital commerce accounts for 13% of total commerce volume — estimated to be more than $3 trillion in 2017 — and will double by 2022. Mobile commerce, which accounts for almost half of digital commerce, is estimated to reach 70% of digital commerce by 2022 (McKinsey, 2018). The increasing trend of electronic transactions, digital commerce growth, and cross-border transactions paves the way for the disproportionate growth of digital payments at an accelerated speed. The key components of digital payments growth also lead to the imperative for banks and other financial institutions to continually develop solutions and innovations enabled by technologies, driven by customer needs and competition (McKinsey, 2018).

Moreover, the dynamics of digital payments development vary across regions and channels. North America has executed more than half of the payment transactions electronically, whereas in China, it has increased to 34% in 2017 due to a 10-fold increase over the last 5 years. The pronounced factor is transaction-based growth arising from the number of transactions moving away from cash — e.g., debit and credit card use has collectively almost doubled over the past five years (McKinsey, 2019). Noticeably, Asia-Pacific, especially China, plays a significant role in accelerating growth and diversifying portfolio of innovative payment solutions due to predominant smartphone adoption, popular online shopping, and technical improvement in network velocity and bandwidth. Although the growth of digital payments in Asia-Pacific and especially China is remarkable, compared to its portion to overall population (two-thirds), digital payments volume in Asia is yet to reach a fair share of the global digital payment transactions. The trend of moving toward real-time, mobile, and in-app payments further fuels growth. There is an increased adoption of mobile app-based payments by merchants and consumers, along with retailers' endeavor in building an omni-channel ecosystem.

This chapter introduces the rise of digital payments, identifies the key drivers of the future trend and growth, and addresses the key challenges that affect the impact, technology, and development of digital payments. As one of the fastest growing engines of global finance revenue, digital payments have gained increasing interest from academia and practitioners. This chapter also examines the major types and key attributes of digital payments and the opportunities and challenges that affect their implementation and success.

6.1 Rise in Digital Payments

Digital payment solutions provide a unified platform to claim payments via an electronic medium when purchases or transactions occur, using various forms of payment instruments that are "cashless" — e.g., debit/credit cards, internet banking, mobile banking, mobile wallets, etc.

The digital payment landscape is crowded, with different payment actors and varied background technologies. New payments solutions with different backgrounds emerge for a common goal to connect payers and payees in an efficient way at a lower cost. Given the rise of ecommerce and greater investment from retailers to enhance the omni-channel ecosystem, new B2B payments and digital checkout are indispensable for the digital commerce ecosystem.

For instance, looking through a typical online shopping consumer journey, when a Singaporean customer purchases on a US online shopping website, bill payment, processing, and authorization were supported by a complex payment value chain. It comprises six key actors that collectively form the digital payment value chain, as shown in Table 6.1 (Deloitte, 2019; PWC, 2016).

- **Customer**: The customer is the end-user who initiates the payment via electronic medium for the purpose of purchase or transaction that includes, but is not limited to, B2B, B2C, and C2C processes and cross-border bill payments for tuition, rent, or

Table 6.1: Types of actors in digital payment value chain and impacts of new payment solutions and alternative payment methods on the participants.

Types of Actors	Impact of New Payment Solutions and Alternative Payment Methods on Actors
Customer	Increasing adoption of new payment solutions among different types of ecommerce processes for services like tracking expenses and loyalty.
Issuer	Leveraging richer credit data, they would expand customer base. Costs to manage risk reduce with higher level of security.
Network	More centralized infrastructure reduces margin but drives volume.
Acquirer	It would reduce switching cost for merchants and provide more value-added services to increase acquisition.
Receiver	It would drive democratization of infrastructure and reduce costs for merchants. More revenue growth generated by tapping on customer data.
Government	It would urge regulation on new technology such as blockchain. More pressure is on keeping pace with complexity and risk associated with privacy, data security and fraud.

Source: Deloitte (2019) and PWC (2016).

any subscriptions. Similarly, loan repayment and investment across borders also grow substantially.

- **Receiver**: The receiver is the merchant or transaction partner who receives the payments from the customer. They pay fees to the acquirer in exchange for its services.
- **Issuer**: The issuer is the bank or financial institution that acquires and engages the customers. They provide payment solutions and underwriting for credit issues.
- **Acquirer**: The acquirer is the financial institution that engages receivers, including merchants. They facilitate the adoption of digital payments on the merchants' end.
- **Network provider**: The network provider clears and settles payments and manages risk in exchange for both the issuer and acquirer.
- **Government**: The regulators who set out rules and regulations that govern the digital payment markets with the objective to foster development and competition and protect the market from potential security risks.

6.2 Drivers of the Digital Payment Trend

Online usage of credit cards and debit cards was first born and widely used because of the lack of alternative payment solutions, and their functionality suited the user needs of browser-based shopping activities. However, alternative payment methods (APMs) and new payment methods thrived because of lower operating costs via agile and cloud-based systems, but more importantly, through the adoption of smartphones and the increasing number of mobile-based transactions. AngelList, a reputed service with the mission of connecting start-ups with investors, lists about 2,556 mobile payment start-ups and around 24,000 investors of interest in the segment with an average estimate of valuation of $4.4 million in USD (AngelList, 2019).

By examining the drivers and underlying fundamentals that drive economy to be digital and cashless, three pronounced factors were identified and highlighted (PWC, 2016), which collectively enable a dynamic and competitive payment market:

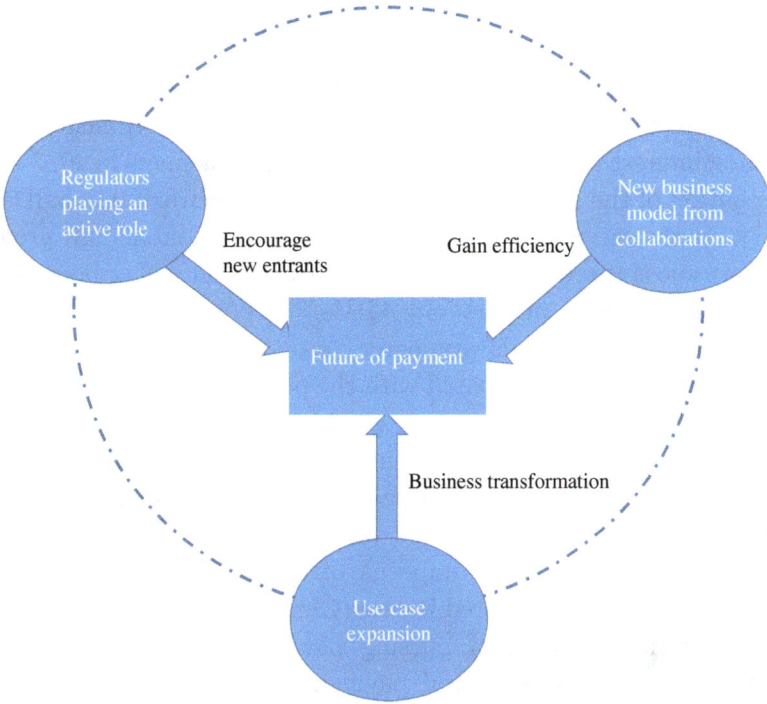

Figure 6.1: Drivers of the future trend and dynamics.

(1) Regulations are being calibrated to encourage new entrants into the digital payment market and adding margin pressures to traditional players' book;

(2) New business models are developed among payment service providers by consolidation and collaboration. Traditional players leverage their established reputations along with strength of new technologies from new payment solutions providers (e.g., social payments) to extend client base with manageable cost;

(3) Extended-use case via new payment solutions (see Figure 6.1).

First, regulation and policy are introduced to reduce market-entry barriers to encourage new payment players to participate in competition and innovation to improve consumer welfare (Kazan and Damsgaard, 2016; BNY Mellon, 2014). On the other hand, regulatory interventions that target traditional card rates emerge as an additional factor that increases pressure on the traditional payment players. For example, Brazil's credit card annual percentage rates (APRs) used to be the highest among the top 20 economies. It fell by 60% due to the targeted regulatory action by the government — i.e., slashing interest rates to alleviate pressure on consumers in 2017 — in the context of the deepest recession witnessed in Brazil (GlobalData, 2017). At the same time, Brazil continues to see double-digit growth in electronic transactions. These facts provide plenty of opportunities to the new payment players and APMs.

Second, as more players enter into the market, the digital payment market gets saturated with the possibilities of synergies and consolidation. The newcomers (e.g., APM start-ups) challenge the prevailing business logic by deconstructing existing payment value streams to their own benefit (Kazan and Damsgaard, 2016). When the existing business model (e.g., payment fee model) becomes less profitable, it leads to the impetus of exploring new products or services that have not existed before (Christensen and Bower, 1996).

In addition, instead of pursing payment fees by approaching payment as a business, digital payment is used largely to provide value-added services to an existing business process (BNY Mellon, 2014). For example, to improve in-store shopping experiences with a smooth checkout service, companies like Walmart and Starbucks embed private-label digital wallets into their digitalization process. Combined with other types of digital wallets (e.g., pass-thru wallets like Apple Pay, closed-loop systems like Alipay and WeChat Pay), collectively they are expected to deliver robust growth through 2022 (McKinsey, 2018).

On the other hand, digital payments as a platform-driven market can be used by businesses to leverage their installed user base to enter other markets. The payment platform owner equip their payers and payees with extended services (e.g., mobile movie ticketing, mobile utility payment) to bridge them into other existing business plat-forms (e.g., ticketing, public utility service) (Kazan and Damsgaard, 2016). The benefit is obvious as entering existing markets is more risk-predictable, with a clearer market size estimate and competitive positioning.

6.3   Challenges of the Digital Payment Trend

It is unlikely (if not impossible) to define a "one size fits all" digital payment strategy as the "end-state" is unrecognizably influenced by fast-evolving technology, changing customer expectations, and shifts in global demographics (BNY Mellon, 2014). Besides, the development and growth of digital payments vary significantly by country and region. First, there are different technologies and infrastructures chosen upon which payment solutions are built. For example, tap-and-go will be predominant in countries with robust near-field communication (NFC) infrastructure (e.g., India, China, Japan). Second, the form of digital payment must serve the value proposition that consumers recognize and accept. In the US and the UK, mobile app use and digital wallet will grow as order-ahead is a way of shopping that is highly valued by consumers. Last but not the least, in an emerging market that lacks infrastructure and first-move advantage in digital payments (e.g., less debit and credit card use), new payment solutions influence how people pay, thereby reshaping the business process in an innovative way (McKinsey, 2018; BNY Mellon, 2014; Bezhovski, 2016).

Despite the gains and prominent growth in these countries, the relative share of digital payments still indicates a huge room for growth. One observation is that digital payments at most comprises low double-digit consumer in-person spending. Lack of ubiquitous merchant acceptance and awareness of consumers on how to use mobile services to make payment remain the main barriers (McKinsey, 2018; BNY Mellon, 2014).

On the contrary, China is known for the ubiquitous adoption of the two dominant payment solutions, WeChat and Alipay, by merchants and consumers. According to the People's Bank of China, prominent growth has been observed in mobile payments from 2013 to 2018, aided by the underlying developments of large ecosystem players (e.g., Alipay, WeChat Pay), which facilitate and profit from retail payments and commercial activities. They tackle a variety of pain points captured from touch points along the consumer journey. For example, Alipay's "cash on delivery" model eases consumers' concerns that sellers would not fulfil the order or the items to be delivered are not up to expectation. Alipay would hold the payment received from consumers and only release to sellers once consumers give a positive rating or default rating without filing any complaint. Alipay began as an escrow service, addressing the fact that many Chinese consumers lacked trust that sellers would fulfil their order. Mobile wallet adoption in China is expected to increase to 60% by 2022 (McKinsey, 2018). However, this growth is tied close to the two Chinese payment ecosystems — WeChat Pay and Alipay — which is a closed-loop system.

Common barriers and challenges are identified through a two-fold categorization — consumers and industry players. For consumers, according to BCG Insights (BCG, 2016), despite their enthusiasm for digital payments, three top concerns still prevent consumers from shifting to digital (Table 6.2).

- **Inertia to use cash**

As noticed in developed and emerging markets, it is not uncommon that consumers are habituated to using cash when making in-store and even online purchase (e.g., UK, China, Japan). The existence of the cash-on-delivery model (e.g., China, Japan), security concerns over digital payment (e.g., prepaid card usage in Japan, such as Suica), and preference of cash for budget management are prominent indicators that a significant portion of consumers hesitate to convert to digital payment (e.g., 70% of Japanese consumers prefer cash over alternative digital payments).

- **Difficulty in using digital payment means**

Product difficulty is considered as a major hurdle for the low adoption of digital payments. Payment service providers have to admit heterogeneity of consumer segments, especially those less evolved with technologies. Instead of creating standards, value propositions, and technologies that confuse the end-users, simplicity of the solution should be comparable to the ease of use of cash to some extent (Sahut, 2008).

Table 6.2: Barriers and challenges facing consumers and service providers.

Participants	Barriers and Challenges
Consumer	• Inertia to use cash • Difficulty to use digital payment means • The lack of compelling value propositions
Service providers	• Regulation leans toward security • Lack justification for infrastructure investment

Source: BCG (2016); PWC (2016).

• The lack of compelling value propositions

To convert consumers into using digital payments, a strong motivation or urge has to be in place to make the consumer feel necessary to adapt. Consumers only resonate with payment products or services that have a clear value proposition, such as having extra benefits or value to gain, or by being influenced by their social circle.

On the other hand, two overarching hurdles were identified by PWC analysis for the industry players, particularly in emerging markets — namely regulation and infrastructure (PWC, 2016).

• Regulation leans toward security

With the recognition of the financial impact of digital payment on the economy, regulators calibrate measures and steps to foster development of digital payments across emerging markets. However, even with such strong motivation, security is still the top consideration when making regulations to prevent fraud, data theft, and credit risk. Thus, it leads to fences built intentionally to block participation from multinational players who are equipped with better technologies and stronger networks. There is a fine line between protection of local environment versus efficiency and growth.

• Infrastructure incomplete in early adoption

In terms of digital infrastructures, emerging economies are finding ways to catch up with developed markets in the area of ATMs and POS machines. However, with low ticket value, it is hard to justify the investment in infrastructure unless it could be offset by transaction volume. In the early stages of digital adoption, a dilemma exists when investment is needed at a low volume of transactions.

Thus, to address these challenges associated with the fast-growing number of solution providers in the digital payments market, namely digital consumer-to-business (C2B) payment ecosystems, FinTechs, and IT companies, the first and the foremost strategy is to tune the value proposition into consumer engagement calls, especially the "tech-savvy" generation. It is time to step back and form a strategic view of payments and their peripheral activities to devise value-added solutions, products, and services. In addition, with the focus on high-growth demographics, e.g., the emerging middle classes in Indonesia and China or previously poorly served segments, e.g., small and medium-sized enterprises (SMEs) or to tackle measures such as India's demonetization move (Kavitha and Kumar, 2018), companies are able to create products and services along the targeted payment flows.

As a following step, accelerating digitalization is inevitable to drive real-time payments with operational efficiencies. Payment plays a significant role in solving pain points for consumers, or delighting them with services beyond expectation. Companies should update technologies and streamline services against internal operational silos. Last but not the least, it is imperative to search for innovative strategic alliances across borders and translate regulatory requirements into competitive advantage. In addition, pursuing non-traditional partnerships with mobile payment service providers or social media operators who enter into the payment market increases the chances of acquiring new customer base, which is otherwise inaccessible.

6.4 Types of Digital Payment

Contextualized in a highly competitive digital payment market, various players have evolved in multiple fronts of advanced technology development. APMs and new payment solutions such as e-wallets and digital currencies play prominent role across markets. As highlighted by multiple evidences and reports (BCG, 2016;

Table 6.3: Global digital payment mix.

Region	Cards	Mobile Wallets	Direct Debit	Bank Transfer	Cash on Delivery	Others
US and Canada	●	◑	○	○	○	◗
Latin America	●	◗	○	◗	○	●
Europe	●	◑	○	◗	○	◑
Asia Pacific	●	◑	○	◗	◗	◗
Africa and Middle East	◑	○	○	○	●	◗

Source: Worldpay (2013).

McKinsey, 2019; PWC, 2016), card transactions are still the most popular payment method in the developed markets. However, many countries and regional markets have recognized the value and benefits of new payment methods or APMs to their economy's growth and showed strong willingness to adopt (e.g., MPesa in Kenya, Alipay in China). According to Worldpay and exemplar academic research, we summarized the prominent digital instruments in different regions and markets (Bezhovski, 2016). The ordinal order of significance of each payment type was marked in moon charts (i.e., crescent, half, gibbous, full moon) as shown in Table 6.3.

- **Credit and debit cards**

Credit and debit cards are still the most popular payment instrument worldwide. Major types of cards include MasterCard, Visa, American Express, Diners Club, Discover, and China Union Pay. The strong usage reflects the preference of millennials and upcoming generations.

- **Mobile wallets**

Mobile wallets are the second most commonly used payment method, except in Africa and Middle East, and are forecast to take over the payment scene, according to Michael Corbat, the CEO of Citigroup. By attaching credit or debit card information to a mobile device, tag-and-go is viable with in-store shopping.

- **Bank transfer**

Bank transfer enabled via internet banking or mobile banking allows money to be withdrawn from one account and transferred to an automated clearing house (ACH) network for clearance before depositing it to the receiver's bank account. This is the third commonly used payment across the markets.

6.5   Technologies Behind the Digital Payment Scene

Behind the digital payment scene, a set of technological advances were identified as a mega-technical trend. It comprises social payments, NFC technology, Bluetooth Low Energy (BLE), and the prominent blockchain technology (PWC, 2016).

- **Social payments**

Social payments are witnessing phenomenal growth along with the boom in social networking services (SNSs) that have introduced their own financial payment instruments. Drawing up on the large existing client base, it is almost natural for SNSs to provide value-added services such as advocating promotions, connecting reviews, and facilitating purchases of consumers' interest. For example, Twitter users are able to pay with tweets. The overall online shopping experiences would be more personalized based on consumers' previous review and purchase records kept in system. This technology movement would reshape payment services and blur the line between commercial and social activities.

- **NFC technology**

NFC technology is known for its safety and convenience, which are highly valued in developing markets. It belongs to the family of short-range wireless connectivity technology that was widely adopted among major mobile phone manufacturers. It allows a mobile phone to embed with a contactless payment card without physical access to users' credit card information.

- **BLE**

BLE technology was mainly used in shopping malls to push promotions to consumers via Bluetooth in store. It also supports in-store payment and peer-to-peer fund transfer within a 50-meter range.

- **Blockchain technology**

Blockchain technology reshapes processing of financial transactions by discarding the traditions of placing ledgers to a single institution. Instead, it encourages the distributed ledger model to improve operational efficiency and realize real-time payment or fund transfer.

6.6 Ingredients for Successful Implementation

Practitioners and academic researchers have prescribed a set of recommendations that are crucial for the success of digital payment strategies and implementations (Deloitte, 2019; PWC, 2016; BCG, 2016; Bezhovski, 2016).

- **Security**

Security was identified as the first priority that concerns consumers when they consider whether to begin their digital payment journey. Continuous improvement in data security and risk management is indispensable to build a trustworthy service and network. This is increasingly important as more cross-border transactions and collaborations among multi-national partners occur.

- **User-centric design**

The key to win over consumers is to make the payment solutions as simple as possible, ideally comparable to the ease of use of cash. Consumers interact with the user interface with multiple layers of underlying protocols and complex technological systems. The inability to make user experience as the main focus would be the major hurdle to drive adoption by the technology-overloaded and distracted new generation of customers.

• **Seamless integration**

Due to the lack of ubiquitous merchant acceptance of digital payments, consumers face the challenge of toggling among multiple payment instruments — cash or cashless. Thus, seamless integration across digital payment gateways through automation and streamlining helps to create a hassle-free payment experience.

6.7   Conclusion

It is foreseeable that a greater convergence of digital payment technologies, consolidations, and collaborations across traditional and new payment solution providers are getting closer. Regulatory framework continues to calibrate to keep pace with the change in the new payment solutions landscape. New business models are generated from a deep understanding of consumer needs. Extensive-use cases and innovative applications of digital payment technologies contribute to economic growth at an accelerated speed. However, to reap the full benefits from the new payment trend, the payment solutions providers are urged to take initiatives to beat inertia to use cash, build trust via robust security mechanisms, and continue investment in technologies with a fine-tuned value proposition in line with the customers' expectations.

References

AngelList (2019). Mobile Payments Startups. Retrieved from https://angel.co/mobile-payments (Accessed 7 July 2020).

BCG (2016). Digital Payments 2020. Retrieved from http://image-src.bcg.com/BCG_COM/BCG-Google%20Digital%20Payments%202020-July%202016_tc m21-39245.pdf (Accessed 7 July 2020).

Z. Bezhovski (2016). The Future of the Mobile Payment as Electronic Payment System. *European Journal of Business and Management*, 8(8), 127–132.

BNY Mellon (2014). Global Payments 2020: Transformation and Convergence. Retrieved from https://www.bnymellon.com/_global-assets/pdf/business-insights/global-payments-2020-transformation-and-convergence.pdf (Accessed 7 July 2020).

C. M. Christensen and J. L. Bower (1996). Customer Power, Strategic Investment, and the Failure of Leading Firms. *Strategic Management Journal*, 17(3), 197–218.

Deloitte (2019). The Future of Digital Payments — Choices to Consider for a New Ecosystem. Retrieved from https://www2.deloitte.com/content/dam/Deloit

te/sg/Documents/financial-services/sg-fsi-future-of-digital-payments.pdf (Accessed 7 July 2020).

GlobalData (2017). The Cards and Payments Industry in Brazil: Emerging Trends and Opportunities to 2020. Retrieved from https://www.researchandmark ets.com/reports/4370753/the-cards-and-payments-industry-in-brazil (Accessed 7 July 2020).

McKinsey & Company (2018). Global Payments 2018: A Dynamic Industry Continues to Break New Ground. Retrieved from https://www.mckinsey. com/~/media/McKinsey/Industries/Financial%20Services/Our%20Insights /Global%20payments%20Expansive%20growth%20targeted%20opportuniti es/Global-payments-map-2018.ashx (Accessed 7 July 2020).

McKinsey & Company (2019). Global Payments Report 2019: Amid Sustained Growth, Accelerating Challenges Demand Bold Actions. Retrieved from https://www.mckinsey.com/~/media/mckinsey/industries/financial% 20services/our%20insights/tracking%20the%20sources%20of%20robust%20 payments%20growth%20mckinsey%20global%20payments%20map/global-payments-report-2019-amid-sustained-growth-vf.ashx (Accessed 7 July 2020).

PWC (2016). Emerging Markets — Driving the Payments Transformation. Retrieved from https://www.pwc.com/gx/en/financial-services/public ations/assets/pwc-emerging-markets-12-July.pdf (Accessed 7 July 2020).

E. Kazan and J. Damsgaard (2016). Towards A Market Entry Framework for Digital Payment Platforms. *Communications of the Association for Information Systems*, 38(1), 761–783.

M. Kavitha and K. S. Kumar (2018). A Study on Digital Payments System With Perspective of Customer's Adoption. *Eurasian Journal of Analytical Chemistry*, 13(SP).

J.-M. Sahut (2008). The Adoption and Diffusion of Electronic Wallets. *Journal of Internet Banking and Commerce*, 13(1), 1–10.

WorldPay (2013). Your Global Guide to Alternative Payments. Retrieved from https://nocash.ro/wp-content/uploads/2014/02/worldpay-alternative-payments-2nd-edition-report.pdf (Accessed 7 July 2020).

Chapter 7

Digital Banks: Igniting Platform Revolution in Banking

Hung Yu-chen

Tech giants are entering the banking sector. In December 2020, the Monetary Authority of Singapore granted digital bank licenses to four new operators. The Digital Full Bank licenses can serve both individual and corporate customers. The two winners in this category are the ride-hailing company, Grab and its consortium with Singapore Telecommunication, and the e-commerce company Sea Ltd, which is the tech giant owning e-commerce platform Shopee, game developer Garena, and digital payments SeaMoney (Monetary Authority of Singapore, 2020). The Digital Wholesale Bank licenses are also granted to serve SMEs and other non-retail sectors. The winners in this category are a consortium led by Greenland Financial Holding Group, and a wholly owned entity by Ant Group Co. Ltd. Out of the four winners, three are digital platforms businesses; Grab (car hailing and food delivery platform), Sea (e-commerce platform), and Ant group (Finance platform). They are expected to start operations by 2022. The future of financial service starts to look a bit different.

Singapore's digital bank framework aims to enable non-bank players with innovative digital business models to offer digital banking services (Monetary Authority of Singapore, 2020). Under this framework, digital bank can take deposits, offer personal loans, issue debit and credit cards, provide insurance, and sell capital market investment products. However, all banking services are to be conducted online. Digital banks will have only one physical place of business operation, with no access to ATMs or cash deposit machine network. Only the cashback services at retail merchants are allowed. This is in stark contrast with traditional banks that offer some banking services via website or mobile apps, but all services can be conducted at the branch with staff assistance.

Singapore is not alone in its advancement in digital banking. As a close rivalry of the Asian financial hub, Hong Kong also issued four more virtual bank licenses in May 2019, bringing the total licenses to eight (Ang, 2020). In the same year, Taiwan also joined the race, issuing its first digital bank license to the social-media-platform–backed Line Bank. These efforts are joining the digital banks already in operation in China (e.g., WeBank, Ant Finance), South Korea (e.g., Kakao Bank), UK (e.g., Monzo, Starling Bank, Revolut), France (e.g., Orange Bank), Canada (e.g., Neo), and the US (e.g., Varo). It is now a common trend to see new digital enterprises entering digital banking. Digital platforms in social media and e-commerce are stepping into the finance sector, which has been traditionally dominated by big banks and financial institutions.

As the new breed of service providers enters the market, consumers have alternative choices to traditional banks. However, most traditional banks already added online banking, mobile apps, and chatbots as digital channels (i.e., e-banking service) to serve customers. Would digital banking be any different to the existing e-services? How would consumers react to digital banking? Could the non-bank players transform banking with their innovative digital business models?

This chapter discusses these questions in five sections. Section 7.1 explains why digital banks are different by comparing and contrasting with digitalized banks. Section 7.2 analyzes what makes consumers embrace digital banking, and what deters their acceptance. Unlike the traditional banks, where consumers can use tangible cues to evaluate service quality, digital banking cannot be evaluated on the same basis. Therefore, Section 7.3 concerns what affects user satisfaction in digital banking.

Part 1: What are Digital Banks	Part 2: Get Them Started	Part 3: Get Them Hooked	Part 4: Get Them All	Part 5: Get Future Proofed
•Why digtial banks are different •Topics •automation •digital maturity •digital advantage •edge on productivity, frictionless customer experience and cost saving	• What makes consumers accept digital banking •Topics •ease of use •perceived usefulness •perceived risks	•What marks customer safisfaction for digital banking •Topics: •generic vs. digital service quality dimensions • e-banking service quality	•Why culture matters •Topics: •Hofstede's culture dimentions •social presence •image concerns	•What changes will the tech giants bring •Topics: •digital platforms business model •network effect •competitive pressure

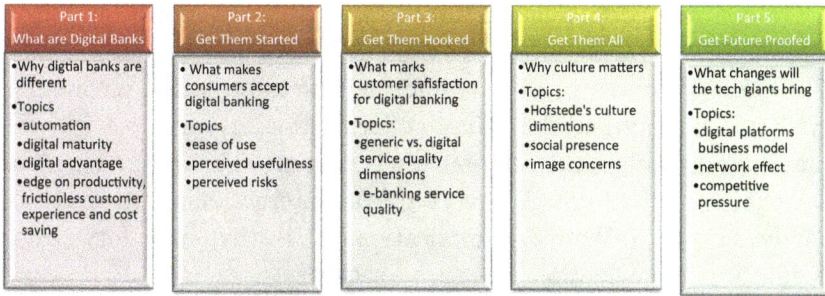

Figure 7.1:   Roadmap.

Digital banks operate in a national context. Culture affects how open consumers are to digital banking. It also affects the service level they expect. We discuss in Section 7.4 how culture plays a role in the adoption of digital banking. More importantly, cultural values inform what is expected in service delivery of digital banking.

Many digital banks are formed by non-bank operators in digital platform business. Digital platforms follow a distinctive business model and rely on the network effect to flourish. Section 7.5 attunes to digital platforms and addresses their motivation to enter the digital banking business. This section concludes the chapter with the changes their innovative business model may bring to the banking sector. The roadmap is illustrated in Figure 7.1.

7.1   Why Digital Banks are Different

Most traditional banks have added online banking, mobile apps, and chatbots as additional channels to serve customers. The electronic delivery of service is termed "digitalized service," in place of manual process previously available at the local branch. Traditional banks are thus "digitalized banks" that offer digitalized banking transformed based on existing operations. They are required to work on a legacy system that requires gradual improvement in order to prevent disruption to current operations. The gradual progression of digital transformation introduces automation in some processes, while some processes are complemented or completed by staff.

In contrast, digital banks are born digital. They are built from scratch for customers to take charge of their finances entirely online. The entire business process is informed by information technology. With full automation, they aim to offer frictionless services with real-time support. Customer relationship is supported by technology from day one. Abundant data is collected from interaction and transaction on devices with Web 3.0 application. It is then put forward to facilitate personalization in future services.

The differences between digitalized banks and digital banks can be better explained through the lens of digital maturity. Digital maturity pertains to a capability to use digital technologies to improve processes, engage talent across the organization, and drive new value-generating business models (Kane *et al.*, 2015). Three categories of companies differing in digital maturity emerged: "early,", "developing," and "maturing." Across industries, an estimated 29% of companies are digitally mature, 45% are developing, whilst 26% are at the early stage (Figure 7.2).

Digital maturity matters because it is the source of digital advantage. Digitally mature companies are significantly more profitable (Westerman *et al.*, 2012). Digitally mature companies generate more revenues from their physical assets, enjoy higher profit margins, and achieve better market valuation.

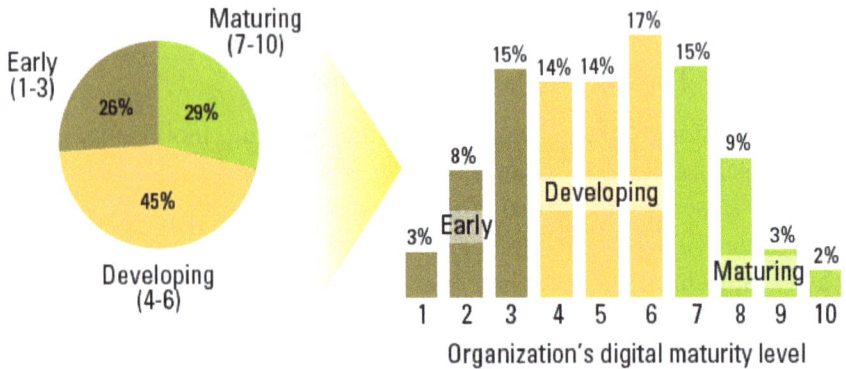

Figure 7.2: To assess companies' digital maturity, respondents from various industries were asked to rate their respective company's digital maturity on a scale from 1 to 10. Three groups emerged: early (26%), developing (45%), and maturing (29%).

Source: Extracted from Kane *et al.* (2015).

To command the digital advantage, enterprises in earlier stages need to overcome significant barriers to move upward to maturity. Along the journey, they are confronted with simultaneous challenges, including a shift of strategic focus, organizational culture, talent development, and leadership. Westerman *et al.* (2012) reported that 35% of companies in the banking sector are considered digitally mature. This means the majority is still in the developing or early stages of digital transformation. Those more advanced in digital transformation are rewarded by the marketing and already command advantage others that still lag behind.

Digital banks are regarded the next frontier of innovation in the financial services sector (Sam, 2019). Born with information technology in their DNA, their entry into the sector lifts the benchmark to a new level. The reason is banking sector, overall, is behind IT and Technology in digital maturity (see Figure 7.3), although it is ahead of industries such as retail, consumer packaged goods, and manufacturing.

Specifically, enterprises in IT and technology lead in using digital technologies to enable employees to work better with customers, partners, and employees. Their employees are better equipped with necessary skill to employees. The leaders in this sector are more advanced in digital capability than other sectors. The management

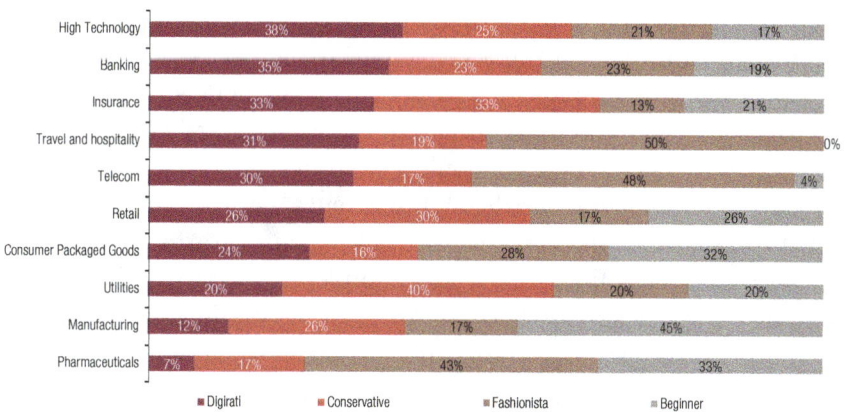

Figure 7.3: Digital maturity breakdown by industry, where the most mature companies are labeled as "Digiterati."
Source: Extracted from Westerman *et al.* (2012).

Sector	Digital maturity [1]	Digital technologies enable employees to work better with:			Select digital qualities				
		Customers	Partners	Employees	Clear strategy	Strategy to transform	Skills provided	Manager encourages use	Leaders have skills
IT and Technology	6.23								
Telecommunications	5.89								
Entertainment, Media	5.49								
Professional Services	5.39								
Transportation, Tourism	5.18								
FSI – Asset Management	5.18								
FSI – Banking	5.14								
Retail	5.03								
Auto	5.01								
Pharma	5.00								
Consumer Goods	4.90								
FSI – Insurance	4.80								
Education	4.71								
Oil & Gas	4.68								
Health Care Provider	4.67								
Manufacturing	4.54								
Public Sector – Federal	4.51								
Construction and Real Estate	4.50								

Top 5 / Bottom 5

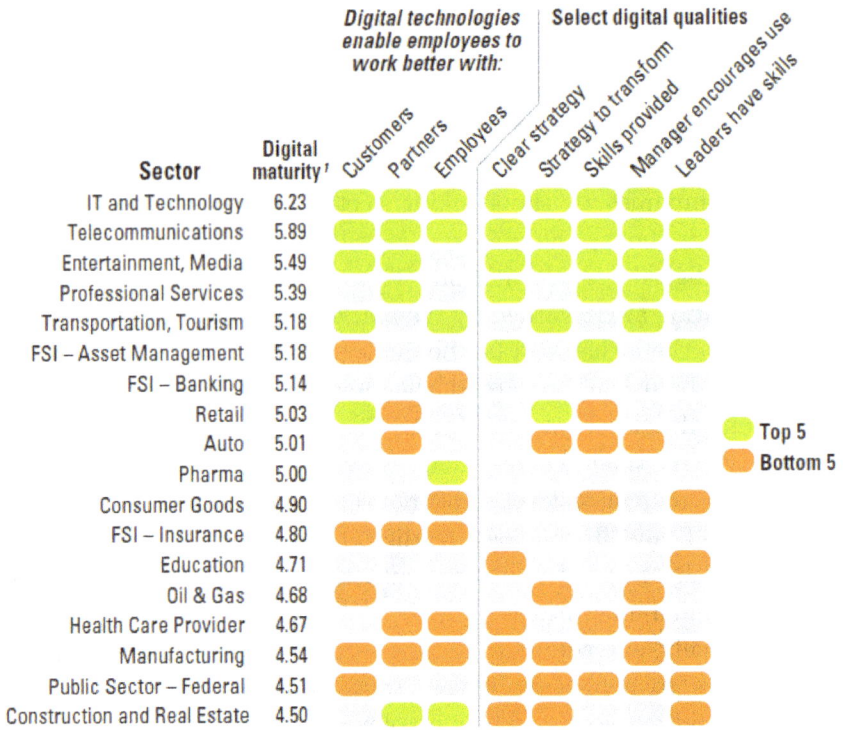

Figure 7.4: Enterprises in IT and technology lead in digital maturity in various fronts.

Source: Figure extracted from Kane *et al.* (2015).

shows encouragement for innovative initiatives and set a clear strategic pathway to continuously overhaul business models (Figure 7.4).

Digital banks based on technology platforms are likely to have an edge on productivity, frictionless customer experience, and cost-saving. By leveraging Artificial Intelligence (AI) to process documents, tasks can be completed in a few minutes, rather than hours or days. Take account opening for example. AI can verify documents submitted by consumers and approve instantly. Whereas, currently, opening an account may require a customer to submit documents online and make a trip to a branch to verify the documents, take deposit and signature, and then issue a copy of account information (Neo, 2020).

Furthermore, digital banks save cost on maintaining physical infrastructure, manpower, and administrative fees. They are in a better position to pass on the cost-saving to customers. In addition, technology is used to innovate and enrich customer experience. For example, digital banks that offer bill-splitting functions can save hassles to transfer the money to the person footing the bill after a group meal. They can also offer promotions and rewards tailored to customer interests, rather than the one-package-for-all kind of promotion.

When most consumers give digital banking a try and get used to the kind of service, they will expect and demand the same seamless services from other service providers. Demanding customers are the ultimate market force to drive future changes. Thus, digital banks are likely to put competitive pressure on traditional banks to expedite digital transformation. Yet, the extent of transformative pressure depends on consumer acceptance of digital banking. If most consumers are hesitant or skeptical about digital banking, digital banks will serve a niche segment on the market. Its impact is limited in this case. Hence, let us turn to consumer acceptance in the next two sections before revisiting the changes digital banks may bring.

7.2   Get Them Started: What Makes Consumers Accept Digital Banking?

According to Technological Acceptance Model, ease of use and perceived usefulness are the main reasons to adopt innovative applications (Straub *et al.*, 1997). With regard to the e-banking services offered by digitalized banks, consumers identify cost-saving and convenience as the two key determinants to whether they use it or not. Lower cost and better convenience contribute to greater perceived usefulness, therefore consumers are more inclined to use e-banking services.

The two factors, cost-saving and convenience, play to the advantage of digital banks. Digital banks are in a position to pass on more savings to users, and they are fast paced to offer novel applications catered to user's lifestyle. Digital banks are likely to be welcomed by consumers if they are able to offer good interface, greater saving, and rich experience to consumers

However, fully automated banking services may worsen feelings of insecurity and create frustration among some consumers, especially when it comes to resolving issues such as erroneous transactions, flawed products, or network problems. Consumer distrust is a major obstacle to taking up electronic delivery of services (Cunningham *et al.*, 2005; Rotchanakitumnuai and Speece, 2003). Distrustful consumers are wearied by the potential to have their financial profiles and transactions misused.

Corroboratively, safety and privacy are shown to be the crucial deterrents to e-banking adoption (Poon, 2008). Moving forward, digital banks will face similar, if not more stringent, scrutiny on safety and privacy. Without safety assurance to gain trust, cheaper fees are associated with higher risk, and convenience is dealt with skepticism that users are easy prey for fraudulent activities.

7.3   Get Them Hooked: What Marks Customer Satisfaction for Digital Banking?

To win trust, reliability is of ultimate importance to digital banking. Reliability is one of the dimensions that consumers use to evaluate service satisfactions. Service satisfaction is the way that digital banks can attract, nurture, and maintain loyal customers. According to the widely accepted SERVQUAL model by Parasuraman *et al.* (1985), service quality falls along five dimensions — *Tangibles, Reliability, Responsiveness, Assurance*, and *Empathy*. The model has shown to be applicable to traditional banks comprising physical branches and e-banking services. In the past, e-banking and traditional banking was regarded as inseparable facets of the banking services, and they are complimentary rather than substitutes channels of service delivery (Wong *et al.*, 2008).

However, digital banks lose tangible cues present in the SERVQUAL model. Digital banking carries ubiquity that the model may not fully accommodate. A separate framework is needed to understand services entirely carried out online. Developed in the context of e-commerce, Alzola and Robaina (2005) specify that

Table 7.1:   Generic vs digital service quality dimensions.

Generic Service Quality Dimensions[a]	Digital Service Quality Dimensions[b]
Tangibles	Design
Appearance of physical facilities, equipment, personnel and communication materials	Intuitive navigation, navigation tools, quick downloading, attractive design, signposting of pages, easy restart and cancellation of the purchase, constant orientation
Reliability	Reliability
Ability to perform the promised service	Correct billing; no not-agreed-upon surcharges; the payment process takes place with no technical hitches
Responsiveness	Guarantee
Willingness to help the user and provide a prompt service	Company interest in dealing with customer complaints and claims; time taken by the company to respond to customer requests by email
Assurance	Security
Knowledge courtesy of employees and their ability to inspire confidence, trust, and credibility	Explanation of the personal data protection policy and mechanisms; explanation of the financial data protection policy and mechanisms; mechanisms used to protect personal and financial data; image of the service provider
Empathy	Personalization
Individualized attention offered to customers	Personalization of products and/or services, payment terms, design; ease of contact

[a]Berry *et al.* (1990).
[b]Alzola and Robaina (2005).

e-service quality dimensions are better captured by *Design, Reliability, Guarantee, Security,* and *Personalization* dimensions. The five dimensions acknowledge the five aspects of SERVQUAL, while accommodating the ubiquity of e-services (see Table 7.1). Thus, it offers a lens for the service dimensions relevant to digital banks, because digital banking shares three similarities to e-commerce: the absence of sales staff, the absence of traditional tangible elements, and customer self-service throughout the service episode.

7.3.1 *Design*

Traditional banks can offer tangible cues to better service quality perception. The outlook of the building, location, office equipment, and appearance of the staff comprise aesthetic cues indicative of professionalism. For digital banks, the perception is solely based on website and app designs. Thus, design is the physical dimension of digital banking. The interface is the starting point for users to interact with, experience, and evaluate a brand. Any deficiency or difficulty in navigation damps consumer confidence.

7.3.2 *Reliability*

Reliability is the ability of a company to perform the promised service. This is the common dimension in the two frameworks. For digital banking, reliability is the most important dimension to win trust. Digital banks should ensure correct billings, no technical glitches, and no hidden fees, so as to earn consumer confidence with error-free processes and transparency.

7.3.3 *Guarantee*

Responsiveness in SERVQUAL refers to the willingness and ability to help users quickly. To demonstrate response capacity, digital banks must engage multiple digital channels to show company interest in dealing with customer complaints and claims. The use of multiple channels can shorten response time by the company to respond to customer inquiries. Unlike e-commerce, where the focus is on handling after-sales problems such as returns, refunds, or sales guarantees, digital banks must safeguard consumers from fraudulent retailers and scammers and assist dispute resolution process.

7.3.4 *Security*

Assurance in SERVQUAL refers to training and courtesy shown by employees and their ability to inspire confidence and credibility. For digital banking, distrustful users show privacy concerns on misuse of consumer's personal and financial data. A clear explanation on data protection helps to reduce uncertainty. In the long run, building an image of integrity with regard to privacy protection earns consumer trust.

7.3.5   *Personalization*

Empathy in SERVQUAL refers to individualized attention to customers. Digital banking is able to obtain abundant information on customers. The data richness allows users to build credit history with the bank and receive personalized rewards, loans, insurance, or matching results with the right retailers. Digital banks should encourage customers to invest time, effort, and money in their platforms by offering differentiated products and services. The personalization will make invested users reluctant to switch.

Among these dimensions, which ones are more important? Recent research on the concept of electronic banking service quality (EBSQ) sheds light on this question. EBSQ refers to "consumers' evaluation of the quality of banking services delivered through internet" (Jun and Cai, 2001). Similar to Alzola and Robaina (2005), the main dimensions of EBSQ include website design, reliability, privacy and security, and customer service and support (Amin, 2016; Ayo *et al.*, 2016). Among these dimensions, Shankar and Jebarajakirthy (2019) suggest reliability and privacy and security are the main reasons for customer loyalty. Website aesthetics are less of a concern among customers. This is because customers use e-banking mainly for ease of transaction and convenience.

7.4   Catch Them All: Why Culture Matters?

Culture is known to exert influences on technology acceptance (Schepers and Wetzels, 2007). Some cultures are faster in accepting technology-based solution than others. Nations with cultural values open to innovation provide a fertile soil for its speedy diffusion. National culture not only affects the extent people are predisposed to accept or reject digital banking but also molds and shapes digital banking according to consumer preference. Technological solutions compatible with cultural values are readily welcomed by the mainstream society. This section discusses cultural influences on diffusion of digital banking based on Hofstede, Geert cultural dimensions and their implications on service design.

In comparisons of national culture, Hofstede developed index scores using data from over 40 countries across 6 dimensions — individualism, power distance, masculinity, uncertainty avoidance, indulgence and long-term orientation (Hofstede, 2001). Nations differ in the six dimensions (see Hofstede-insights.com [n.d.] for updated index scores).

Among these dimensions, uncertainty avoidance (UAI) shows the strongest linkage to innovation acceptance. UAI describes the degree to which individuals are threatened by uncertain situations. In cultures highly avoidant of uncertainty, people show low tolerance to risk, unpredictability, and ambiguity. Most people only trust a new technological application after observing its successful use by other people.

Countries with high uncertainty avoidance tend to take a longer time to accept new technology. UAI affects the propensity to use e-commerce (Al-kailani and Kumar, 2011), e-service (Sabiote *et al.*, 2012), and digital platforms, such as Airbnb (Muñoz-Leiva *et al.*, 2018). Therefore, nations with a high UAI index are expected to be slower to introduce digital banking into the banking system. Once introduced, it has a higher chance for digital banking to take a long time to penetrate the market.

In contrast, individualism has shown to have a positive effect on innovation adoption (He and Lee, 2020). Individualism describes the extent to which people view themselves as being independent from other people (Triandis *et al.*, 1988). Individualists value autonomy, independence, and self-reliance. They are assertive of own value judgment and seek to be defiant of social influences. Therefore, they look for uniqueness, rather than social approval, in their decision-making. Since digital banking offers greater value, self-service, and personalization, these characteristics are valuable to individualists. Individualism is compatible with digital banking.

On the contrary, power distance and masculinity are expected to have an adverse effect on adoption of digital banking. Power distance dimension describes the acceptance that power is distributed unequally. Masculinity dimension refers to a preference in society for achievement, heroism, assertiveness, and material rewards for success. Societies high in power distance and masculinity show a propensity to prefer face-to-face communication over digitally mediated communication tools (Straub *et al.*, 1997). People in high-power-distance and masculine cultures look to social cues in communication. They are attentive to social cues in order to affirm a higher social hierarchy or a superior sense of success. They have a higher expectation on social presence in service. Automated services do not fit well with their needs and expectations.

The adverse effects due to cultural values can be mitigated with thoughtful calibration of social presence in the platform. Digital-mediated communication tools nowadays can permeate social presence to a large extent, such as identifying posture, facial expression, and attire. Their deployment can match with consumer expectations. For example, Asian cultures are service-oriented, and customers are used to high service standard supported by attentive staff. Self-services are not associated with high social prestige. Consumers in culture of high power distance also expect to feel that customer is king. Therefore, the "human touch" indicative of superiority in social hierarchy is likely to be appreciated. For instance, VIP customers are entitled to enjoy teleconferencing and priority staff support.

In summary, how to engineer "human touch" in digital banking platform requires strategic thinking on positioning in the market. A strong focus on utilitarian benefits, such as low cost or convenience, may limit its appeal to market segments that do not mind to be associated with budget or cheap image. Alternatively, social presence can be deployed strategically to address image concerns. Image concerns refer to the degree that the use of the innovation is seen as enhancing to one's image or social status. Consumers are more likely to adopt digital banking when using it enhances self-image or social image (van Slyke *et al.*, 2010). Positioning along a smart and sleek image is more likely to echo well with most users. This positioning requires strategic considerations to balance service features and cultural values.

7.5 Get Future-Proofed: What Changes Will Tech Giants Bring?

Some digital banks are formed by established digital platforms. Digital platforms refer to businesses connecting external members of communities to enable them to interact or transact (Reillier and Reillier, 2017). Unlike traditional organizations, they do not run as linear pipes that use their linear value chains to transform inputs (e.g., deposits) into outputs (e.g., loans) and earn a profit for their value-adding goods/services. Instead, digital platforms create value by acting as economic catalyst that enables value-creating interactions between users (Evans *et al.*, 2011). Despite the differences in core businesses, digital platforms are commonly nimble, scalable, and light in physical assets (see Figure 7.5 for types of platforms).

Digital platforms have already significantly disrupted industries dominated by pipeline businesses, such as hotels, publishing, and taxi services. The same trend started in finance. Blockchain technology

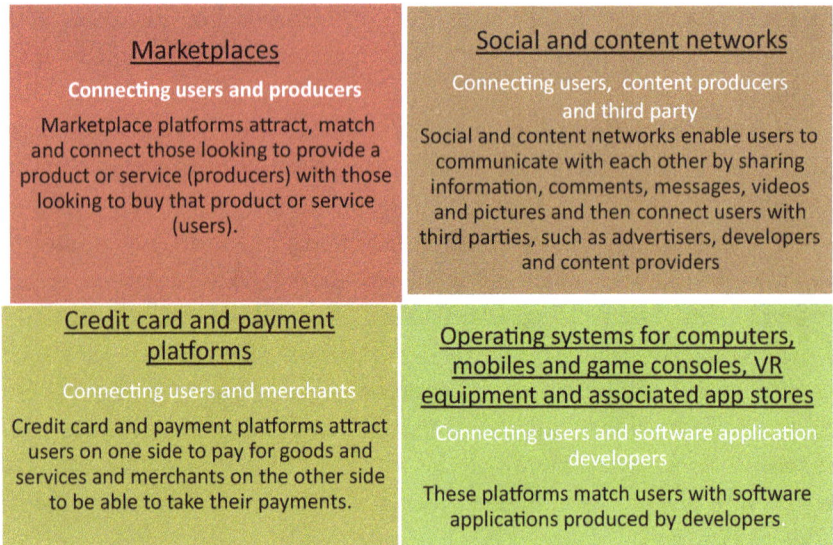

Marketplaces	Social and content networks
Connecting users and producers	Connecting users, content producers and third party
Marketplace platforms attract, match and connect those looking to provide a product or service (producers) with those looking to buy that product or service (users).	Social and content networks enable users to communicate with each other by sharing information, comments, messages, videos and pictures and then connect users with third parties, such as advertisers, developers and content providers
Credit card and payment platforms	Operating systems for computers, mobiles and game consoles, VR equipment and associated app stores
Connecting users and merchants	Connecting users and software application developers
Credit card and payment platforms attract users on one side to pay for goods and services and merchants on the other side to be able to take their payments.	These platforms match users with software applications produced by developers.

Figure 7.5: Types of Platform Business Models according to the communities they connect.
Source: Based on Reillier and Reillier (2017).

enables bitcoin and other cryptocurrencies to be alternative payment platforms bypassing current bank transfer networks. Crowdfunding platforms, such as lending club and Kickstarter, become popular marketplaces to seek public funding without resorting to business loans or equity market.

Now social network sites and e-commerce are entering digital banking to their business model. Platforms are motivated to do so, because digital banking business is a spoke that spins the whirlwind of network effects. Network effect refers to the impact that the number of users of a platform has on the value created for each users (Parker and van Alstyne, 2005). A platform becomes more valuable when more people use it. Digital banking is a service that increases stickiness of the users.

For example, an e-commerce platform can offer loans to participating merchants based on their transaction record. These participating merchants may not have a scale to obtain loans from the banks. By providing loans to participating merchants, the e-commerce platform motivates merchants to sell more through it rather than a competing platform, because the merchants know they are building credit worthiness. When there are more merchants on the supply side, the platform becomes more attractive to consumers on the demand side. More frequent transactions generate more revenue for the platform.

Consumers are motivated to deposit money in an e-commerce site to facilitate buying. While consumers deposit money solely to spend on the e-commerce site, the e-commerce site becomes more attractive to merchants. More types of products and services (e.g., insurance products) will join the site. An expansion on the supply-side draws in more customers. The digital banking service supports the e-commerce site expansion via maximizing cross-side network effect. That is, the network effect created by users from one side of the market on the users from the other side of the market.

The incorporation of pipeline business into platform is a common strategy among large companies. Most large companies, such as Amazon, Google and Facebook, complement their platform business with non-platform offerings. For example, Amazon started as an e-commerce retailer for books, using Internet as an outlet to distribute books (i.e., Amazon Retail). It then transformed to be an e-commerce platform for book retailers, and gradually everything else (i.e., Amazon Marketplace). It offered pipeline services to facilitate the users on the platforms — Prime for consumers and Fulfillment by Amazon (FBA) for merchants to pick pack and ship products to consumers. This mix of platform business with pipeline services delivers the best experience to distinctive communities.

Platform businesses can be ultra-competitive because they can afford to subsidize digital banking. It has been shown that multisided platforms can lose money continuously on one side of the market, as long as the loss in one side can be covered by revenue from another side of the market. It is the aggregation of revenues from multiple sides of platform that sustains their business model (Rochet and Tirole, 2003). By the same token, platform businesses can subsidize digital banking service, as long as they are generating revenues from other transactions. They can offer services at a low fee, or no fee, which most digitalized banks find it hard to match.

Digitalized banks work via a pipeline business model where they take deposits and earn interests from giving loans, and charged account or service fees. When more people are transacting, depositing, and borrowing from digital banks, they do so less with digitalized banks. Most digitalized banks offer credit cards. In the past, e-commerce platforms need to issue credit card with banks to encourage spending with rewards. Once the e-commerce platforms have their own digital banking, they can offer rewards in favor of payment using own services. In this way, they collect more data and become more accurate in predictive analytics. Taken together, traditional banks can expect their business to be cannibalized by digital banks.

In addition, digital banks can tap into more people to deposit money with them. Consumers who do not have bank accounts or credit card can still be their customers. The underserved market segments are now accessible by digital banks. For them, digital payment becomes the norm, and they will expect all banking services to have a similar level of accessibility and automation.

So tech giants want to be your banks. Will they make a splash? Digital banks backed by platforms business models can tap into new sources of supply. Their digital capability enables new consumption behavior and innovates the way that credit is assessed. They are coming, staying and, most likely, altering the landscape of banking altogether.

References

L. M. Alzola and V. P. Robaina (2005). Servqual: Its Applicability in Electronic Commerce B2C. *Quality Management Journal*, 12(4), 46–57. https://doi.or g/10.1080/10686967.2005.11919270

M. Al-Kailani and R. Kumar (2011). Investigating uncertainty avoidance and perceived risk for impacting internet buying: a study in three national cultures. *International Journal of Business and Management*, 6(5), 76–92.

M. Amin (2016). Internet Banking Service Quality and Its Implication on e-customer Satisfaction and e-customer Loyalty. *International Journal of Bank Marketing*. https://doi.org/10.1108/IJBM-10-2014-0139

P. Ang (2020). Singapore to Have 4 Digital Banks, with Grab-Singtel and Sea Getting Digital Full Bank Licences. Banking News & Top Stories - *The Straits Times*, December 4. Retrieved from https://www.straitstimes. com/business/banking/mas-awards-digital-full-bank-licences-to-grab-singtel-and-sea-ant-gets-digital

C. k. Ayo, A. A. Oni, O. J. Adewoye and I. O. Eweoya (2016). E-banking Users' Behaviour: e-Service Quality, Attitude, and Customer Satisfaction. *International Journal of Bank Marketing*. https://doi.org/10.1108/IJBM-12-2014-0175

L. L. Berry, V. A. Zeithaml and A. Parasuraman (1990). Five Imperatives for Improving Service Quality. *Sloan Management Review*, 31(4), 29–38.

L. F. Cunningham, J. Gerlach and M. D. Harper (2005). Perceived Risk and e-banking Services: An Analysis From the Perspective of the Consumer. *Journal of Financial Services Marketing*. https://doi.org/10.1057/palgrave .fsm.4770183

D. S. Evans and R. Schmalensee, M. D. Noel, H. H. Chang and D. D. Garcia-Swartz (2011). Platform Economics: Essays on Multi-sided Businesses. In D. S. Evans (Ed.), *Platform Economics: Essays on Multi-sided Businesses* (Competition Policy International). https://ssrn.com/abstract=1974020

M. He and J. Lee (2020). Social Culture and Innovation Diffusion: A Theoretically Founded Agent-based Model. *Journal of Evolutionary Economics*. https:// doi.org/10.1007/s00191-020-00665-9

Hofstede-insights.com. (n.d.). Compare Countries — Hofstede Insights. Retrieved from https://www.hofstede-insights.com/product/compare-coun tries/ (Accessed February 6, 2021).

G. H. Hofstede (2001). Culture's Consequences, Second Edition: Comparing Values, Behaviors, Institutions and Organizations Across Nations (Sage Publications, Inc, Thousand Oaks, CA).

M. Jun and S. Cai (2001). The Key Determinants of Internet Banking Service Quality: A Content Analysis. *International Journal of Bank Marketing*. https://doi.org/10.1108/02652320110409825

G. C. Kane, D. Palmer, A. N. Phillips, D. Kiron and N. Buckley (2015). Strategy, not Technology, Drives Digital Transformation, Becoming a digitally mature enterprise [Online]. *MIT Sloan Management Review*. http://sloanreview.mit.edu/projects/strategy-drives-digital-transformation/

Monetary Authority of Singapore (2020). MAS Announces Successful Applicants of Licences to Operate New Digital Banks in Singapore. Retrieved from https://www.mas.gov.sg/news/media-releases/2020/mas-announces-successful-applicants-of-licences-to-operate-new-digital-banks-in-singapore (Accessed February 6, 2021).

F. Muñoz-Leiva, X. Mayo-Muñoz, X. and A. De la Hoz-Correa (2018). Adoption of Homesharing Platforms: A Cross-Cultural Study. *Journal of Hospitality and Tourism Insights*. https://doi.org/10.1108/jhti-01-2018-0007

Neo (2020). Digital Banking vs. Digitized Banking, November 12. Retrieved from https://www.neofinancial.com/posts/digitized-banking-vs-digital-banking

A. Parasuraman, V. A. Zeithaml and L. L. Berry (1985). A Conceptual Model of Service Quality and Its Implications for Future Research. *Journal of Marketing*. https://doi.org/10.2307/1251430

G. G. Parker and M. W. Van Alstyne (2005). Two-sided Network Effects: A Theory of Information Product Design. *Management Science*. https://doi.org/10.1287/mnsc.1050.0400

W. C. Poon (2008). Users' Adoption of e-banking Services: The Malaysian Perspective. *Journal of Business and Industrial Marketing*. https://doi.org/10.1108/08858620810841498

L. C. Reillier and B. Reillier (2017). *Platform Strategy: How to Unlock the Power of Communities and Networks To Grow Your Business* (Routledge; Taylor & Francis).

J. C. Rochet and J. Tirole (2003). Platform Competition in Two-Sided Markets. *Journal of the European Economic Association*. https://doi.org/10.1162/154247603322493212

S. Rotchanakitumnuai and M. Speece (2003). Barriers to Internet Banking Adoption: A Qualitative Study Among Corporate Customers in Thailand. *International Journal of Bank Marketing*. https://doi.org/10.1108/02652320310498465

C. M. Sabiote, D. M. Frías and J. A. Castañeda (2012). The Moderating Effect of Uncertainty-Avoidance on Overall Perceived Value of a Service Purchased Online. *Internet Research*. https://doi.org/10.1108/10662241211214557

K. W. Sam (2019). Digital Banks Get Real in Singapore. Retrieved from https://www.pwc.com/sg/en/publications/digital-banks-get-real-in-singapore.html

J. Schepers and M. Wetzels (2007). A Meta-analysis of the Technology Acceptance Model: Investigating Subjective Norm and Moderation Effects. *Information and Management.* https://doi.org/10.1016/j.im.2006.10.007

A. Shankar and C. Jebarajakirthy (2019). The Influence of e-banking Service Quality on Customer Loyalty: A Moderated Mediation Approach. *International Journal of Bank Marketing.* https://doi.org/10.1108/IJBM-03-2018-0063

D. Straub, M. Keil and W. Brenner (1997). Testing the Technology Acceptance Model Across Cultures: A Three Country Study. *Information and Management,* 33(1), 1–11. https://doi.org/10.1016/S0378-7206(97)00026-8

H. C. Triandis, R. Bontempo, M. J. Villareal, M Asai and N. Lucca (1988). Individualism and Collectivism: Cross-Cultural Perspectives on Self-Ingroup Relationships. *Journal of Personality and Social Psychology.* https://doi.org/10.1037/0022-3514.54.2.323

C. van Slyke, H. Lou, F. Belanger and V. Sridhar (2010). The Influence of Culture on Consumer Oriented Electronic Commerce Adoption. *Journal of Electronic Commerce Research,* 11(1), 30–40.

G. Westerman, M. Tannou, D. Bonnet, P. Ferraris and A. McAfee (2012). The Digital Advantage: How Digital Leaders Outperform Their Peers in Every Industry. *Capgemini Consulting and The MIT Center for Digital Business,* pp. 1–24.

D. H. Wong, N. Rexha and I. Phau (2008). Re-examining traditional service quality in an e-banking era. *International Journal of Bank Marketing,* 26(7), 526–545. http://dx.doi.org/10.1108/02652320810913873

Chapter 8

Digital Transformation of Banks: The Case of DBS

Tay Kok Choon and Calvin M. L. Chan

The digital economy has redefined the way people do business, and banking is no exception. Established banks are experiencing tough competition. Global technology companies are looking to disrupt the banking business. These agile technology companies, with the potential to emerge as digital banks, are actively expanding their product portfolio, capitalizing on their deep technical expertise while aggressively seeking collaboration opportunities to invest in more customer-centric products.

On June 28, 2019, the Monetary Authority of Singapore (MAS) announced that it would grant up to five new digital bank licenses. This was on top of any digital banks that the local banking institutions might want to set up in accordance with the existing Internet banking framework (MAS, 2019). This development is significant as it opens the playing field to non-banking entities. Subsequently, in its August 2019 publication, "Digital Banks Get Real in Singapore," PwC commented that "digital banks are catalyzing change across the global banking sector with their keen focus on hyper-personalization, adoption of new technologies and the willingness to embrace new business models." Regarding the new licenses to be issued by MAS, it observed that the focus was not just on the "underserved or unbanked market segments, for example SMEs and millennials" but it would provide "further impetus for existing banks to accelerate the innovation of their digital offerings" (PwC, 2019).

The MAS' decision to nurture growth in the digital banking arena should come as no surprise considering how technology has advanced and particularly, how smartphones and other mobile devices have become a huge part of people's lives. This, in turn, has prompted internet providers to raise their game and ensure increased and seamless mobile connectivity, which then feeds and defines the users' expectations. As PwC (2019) puts it:

> ··· *the financial services sector is transforming. Amid the explosion of data through a wide variety of sources, the use of advanced data analytics and machine learning promises to unlock deeper and richer insights into customers' financial needs. Customers are expecting more: greater access, better accessibility, more integrated experience, addressing their global/regional needs and integrating personal and business financial needs.* (p. 3)

To keep up with the times and in an effort to retain and grow their pool of customers, established banks need to change their traditional way of doing business. They are "digitalizing their core business processes, reassessing organizational structures, and retraining internal talent to brace for the future" (PwC, 2019). DBS Bank Limited is one such financial institution that has made a great leap forward in this respect.

8.1 DBS' Digital Journey

Established in 1968, DBS Bank Limited is a leading banking and financial services group in Asia with branches in 18 markets. Listed and headquartered in Singapore, DBS has made its presence felt in the three key Asian "axes of growth": Greater China, Southeast Asia, and South Asia. The bank's credit ratings — "AA-" from Moody's and "Aa1" from Standard & Poor's — are among the highest in the world (DBS, 2018b; Grant, 2018). To strengthen its presence and reach across the Asian markets, DBS formulated a strategy to put technology at the core of its banking business. From 2010 to 2014, the bank spent S$600 million annually on technology. An additional

S\$200 million was also committed for the following three years (Tan, 2014).

As part of its digital transformation (DT) journey, the bank's technology infrastructure was revamped. Workspaces were redefined to encourage new ideas. Working with their startup partners, DBS introduced hackathons on a regular basis to "find teams with creative concepts that would make banking effortless, so customers could focus more on the things that matter to them" (DBS, 2019b). The teams that outperform the rest could land a job with the banking group.

DT had delivered dividends for DBS. Recognized for its global leadership, it has been named "World's Best Digital Bank" by *Euromoney*, "Global Bank of the Year" by *The Banker*, and "Best Bank in the World" by *Global Finance*, making it the third year in a row (2018–2020). In addition, DBS' track record as "Safest Bank in Asia" has been unbeaten for 12 consecutive years as it retained this award by *Global Finance* from 2009 to 2020 (DBS, 2020).

In terms of business strategies, given the bank's strong Asian heritage, DBS remained focused on Asia, thereby giving them the advantage and edge. In April 2016, DBS launched its digibank services in India. It is India's first mobile-only, branchless, paperless, and signatureless bank. The digital platform allows for opening of a digibank account via an app on a mobile phone and performing biometric verification at the customers' convenience. Customer service was delivered through an artificial intelligence (AI)-driven virtual assistant, and security was assured using a dynamic soft token security system embedded in the customer's smartphone. This was deemed to be more secured than imputing one-time passwords received via SMS. Through the digibank initiative, DBS was able to add 100,000 customers a month (Hartung, 2017) and as of March 2019, had up to 2.5 million customers (DBS, 2019a). They took the same idea and transplanted it to Indonesia, achieving similar success. Digitalization has clearly expanded the bank's customer base and enabled DBS to better service their customers and at the same time reduce their servicing cost, thereby improving the bank's margin.

8.1.1 *Gupta at the Helm*

There are no boundaries in digital banking. It enabled DBS to capture new markets, accelerating its growth to be Southeast Asia's largest bank. And that was the path that its CEO, Piyush Gupta, has set the banking group on. In Gupta's own words on his Twitter account (Speculand, 2020):

> *If you want to compete you must embrace technology. Which means not just the technology change but a culture change, take risk, being willing to experiment, be nimble, be focused on the customer, be data driven, be obsessed with continuous change.*

When Gupta joined the bank as its CEO in November 2009, he believed that the bank's potential had not been met. His vision was to transform it into a world-class multinational bank. He envisaged that with a compelling strategy, an effective and efficient operational architecture, and a performance culture, the bank could improve multifold. In early 2010, under his leadership, DBS formalized and communicated its strategic vision to be the Asian bank of choice for the New Asia, and it would have a presence in Southeast Asia, Greater China, and South Asia (DBS, 2010). On home soil, DBS would continue to offer the entire suite of banking services, but outside of Singapore, the bank would focus on corporate, SME, and affluent banking.

From 2014 to 2018, DBS embarked on a DT journey. The organization chose a path that involved redefining the company's strategy; rebuilding capabilities; and experimenting with new processes, and adopting and scaling up, if successful. It entailed changes across multiple parts of the bank's operation at the same time. What inspired Gupta on the need for such a significant transformation were three things. First, he observed how Alibaba was redefining banking in substantially different ways and sensed that the banking business was facing existential threats and loss of revenue. Thus, there was a need for DBS to proactively change its core to stay in business. Second, his previous experience at Citibank made him aware of the need to position DT as a "mainstream" exercise, otherwise it would be a futile endeavor. Lastly, through his elderly father, he witnessed first-hand human adaptability to a changing environment and understood the kind of environment needed to facilitate change (Grant, 2018).

In May 2018, DBS launched its "Live More, Bank Less" campaign. The objective was to make the bank invisible in such a way that when customers used any or all of the bank's services, it would be second nature to them. To DBS, if the customer could enjoy life more and spend less time on the chore and the hassle of banking, then that would be an ideal kind of banking outcome to create (DBS, 2018b; Yahya, 2016).

8.1.2 *Leadership is the Linchpin*

To ensure the bank's DT success, Gupta devoted 100% of his time to drive the change. He galvanized the support of his Board, which agreed to provide major budget commitments over several years for the transformation effort. He aligned the bank's C-suite, management staff, and everybody within the organization to support this significant transformation. He led DBS staff to believe that taking calculated risk was tolerable and was encouraged. This cultural change gained huge traction across the entire organization and resulted in a fundamental mindset change that encouraged DBS staff to operate like a startup, creating many innovations that enhanced the bank's operations. DBS became obsessed with satisfying customers' needs and being data-driven and agile. The culture of experimentation permeated the entire organization. In short, the freedom to experiment with new things unleashed the creativity of the employees. As Gupta noted:

> *I found that once you give people permission and you give them some training; you unleash this tremendous energy to do things. ⋯ My first two years [here] I used to run projects top-down. The last couple of years I've been blown away with what people are doing. Everybody is driving this transformation and change in every part of the company.* (Grant, 2018)

Technology architecture changes feature prominently in DBS' DT. Technology architecture "describes the infrastructure required to support applications, operations, and reporting requirements"

(Rosen *et al.*, 2000). It also refers to the "framework for building an enterprise including networking, hardware, operating systems, database management systems, and application development standards" (Mccord and Boone, 2008). This meant that DBS had to change its competitive frame and start thinking like a tech company and responding in such a manner as well. They started looking at what other tech companies were doing and aimed to model themselves after them. David Gledhill, the bank's Chief Information Officer and Group Head of Technology and Group Operations until July 2019, came up with GANDALF — Google, Amazon, Netflix, Alphabet, LinkedIn, Facebook — with the "D" referring to DBS.

However, to become the "D" in GANDALF, it was not just technology. Gupta embraced Harvard professor Clayton Christensen's theory of "jobs to be done" which is basically thinking about the customer journey and understanding customer behavior (Christensen *et al.*, 2016). Utilizing DBS' own four Ds — discover, define, develop, and deploy — journey methodology, the bank reimagined what the customer really wants. Everyone in DBS is trained in the four Ds and embraces this journey on how to be customer-centric.

With DT under Gupta's leadership, DBS' organizational capabilities transformed in multiple ways. They no longer acquired customers like before because they were inspired by the way Amazon, Facebook, and Alibaba's Ant Financial did it. These companies had no physical stores and no people on the streets but their customer base grew at warp speed. On Singles' Day — 11 November — in 2016, Ant Financial gave "100 million consumers credit and approved 1.33 million loans worth 50 billion yuan" (Lim, 2017). This is equivalent to about US$7 billion or S$10 billion, the amount in loans DBS handled in an entire year!

Instant fulfillment became DBS' new mantra. The bank no longer needed multiple days or even hours to complete a transaction. Processes were redesigned to impress customers with the bank's responsiveness and efficiency. Using data, DBS moved from cross-sell to cross-buy as it endeavored to give customers multiple choices under different conditions. The shift from push to pull marketing came across as more appealing to DBS' target customers.

DBS changed its mindset to focus on collaboration and partnerships and see these two aspects as integral elements in growing their business. It no longer relied solely on its own pipelines but tried to be more effective in utilizing its platforms to grow revenue.

Like the maestro of a great orchestra, Gupta conducted DBS' DT by figuring out a way to harness digital technology into a coherent set of strategy-based initiatives that had the best potential of an enterprise-wide impact. He then rallied the organization from top to bottom to buy into these initiatives, encouraged them to bring prototypes to reality, and if they were successful, adopted and scaled these implementations so as to reap the full benefits of the transformation effort.

8.2 DBS DT Strategy

8.2.1 *Leveraging the Power of Data*

Moving beyond intuition or opinions, DBS actively promoted a management culture based on evidence, facts, and numbers. Data analytics enabled the bank to reduce costs, better understand its customers, and identify business opportunities. It allowed DBS to better anticipate loan defaults and uncover customers who are underpaying for their products and services. The bank no longer relied solely on the personal networks of its bankers to prospect for new customers. With data mining, it analyzed payment networks to find non-customers who were affiliated with their current customers, as well as elicited the profiles of their best customers and used reverse-lookup to find prospects with similar profiles (Sia *et al.*, 2016).

DBS' customer call centers handle several million calls each year. Digitalizing these call centers helped the bank to deliver a better customer experience. The use of data analytics helped the bank to create targeted customer service that was more effective. In addition, chatbots and guided conversations helped to "automate and streamline real-time interactions with customers, as well as keep service delivery seamless and available 24/7" (IMDA, 2018). This resulted in a "50% reduction of queue times and saved 100 million customer hours" (IMDA, 2018). One of the ways they were able to achieve this early on in their digital journey, was to employ the use of call predictions.

> *DBS used call predictions to pre-empt the nature of customers' calls to their customer service officers (CSOs). By analysing patterns of recent incidents faced by the customers, DBS was able to predict the nature of the calls and quickly identify all relevant information without requiring the customers to provide any information. The CSOs were thus able to reduce call handling time and offer quick resolutions to the customer's problem.* (IMDA, 2018)

From call prediction, the bank went one step further, moving beyond call management and problem resolution. It analyzed its customers' behaviors as well as key events so that it could redesign its processes and measures in an effort to proactively enhance the customer journey experience (IMDA, 2018). One example can be seen in how their systems have been set up to deal with fairly run-of-the-mill potential problems such as when they detected a failed credit card transaction. A process was set up to analyze possible reasons for this. In the event the reason was that the customer had not activated a new credit card, the system would pre-emptively send the customer an SMS message with the reason why the recent transaction had not been accepted as well as steps to resolve the issue. The idea is for the customer to have the means to rectify the situation immediately and retry to make the purchase, thus achieving the original sought-after conclusion, all without having to contact the call center for lengthy phone engagements. Thus, by using analytics and chatbots, DBS was able to "customize their digital service to each customer" so that they could "easily access a whole array of services and any issues they face (could) be resolved effortlessly and quickly" (IMDA, 2018).

Data optimization was also extended to the bank's network of ATMs, and this helped to streamline some of the processes that were already in place, which in turn was beneficial for the bank's bottom line. Utilizing data analytics and sensors embedded in each ATM for machine-to-machine (M2M) communication, DBS was able to "accurately predict ATM usage and customer withdrawal patterns for each machine." With this information, the bank was able to schedule its cash reloading times at non-peak periods, i.e., at times when it knew there would be fewer customers who wanted to use the machines. This translated to a reduction of 350,000 customers being affected by cash reloading each year as well as a reduction in its ATM cash-outs by more than 90%. It also meant that fewer trips — reduced by 10% — were required to reload the ATMs as well as less leftover cash — decreased by 30% — was returned to the bank (Sia *et al.*, 2016).

8.2.2   *Focusing on Process Improvement*

DBS was ranked last among the top five local banks in Singapore in the 2009 Annual Customer Satisfaction Index published by the Singapore Management University. Paul Cobban, the bank's Chief Operating Officer of Technology and Operations, was tasked to reverse this trend. Introducing a process improvement event (PIE) methodology, he set out to streamline the poorly defined but strictly structured internal processes throughout the bank. Each PIE takes five days to complete and had a number of well-defined steps comprising current-state mapping, a waste walk, future-state mapping, an action plan, documentation, and an out-brief. At the end of an event, the team was able to eliminate waste and cut a certain number of customer hours from that process. Between 2009 and 2013, DBS staff completed 184 PIEs, resulting in savings of more than 230 million "customer hours."

8.2.3   *Focusing on Customer Journeys*

The silo approach that DBS traditionally offered is no longer relevant in today's context. Customers are seeking a seamless and integrated solution to their banking needs and not a series of products. In the face of new competition, customer retention has become their priority. To this end, DBS has successfully embarked on a DT journey that has enabled them to move from being product-centric to customer-centric. Its goal was to "foster a mindset shift that would go beyond developing a culture of customer service excellence to creating a culture of digitally enabling new customer experiences" (Sia *et al.*, 2016).

David Gledhill gives one an example: DBS Paylah! Launched in 2014, this is a mobile digital wallet that can be used for a various activities such as to pay bills, buy items, donate to charity, and even send red packets during festive occasions. This was how the bank took customer experiences to a new level (Choudhury, 2015).

DBS established a customer journey design laboratory in 2013. This allowed the staff to map the customer experiences, put themselves in the customers' shoes, and seek to understand issues encountered by customers across multiple touchpoints. From this perspective, the staff think about what other banking services could be offered to customers in the digital-enabled context (Sia *et al.*, 2016). As Neal Cross, DBS' Chief Innovation Officer until January 2019, explains: "We consider what they are thinking, what are their emotions, what is their experience, what they are concerned about, and then try and improve that process so their journey is more joyful" (Paperny, 2015).

The design of new customer-centric experiences was guided by customers' needs and a set of core Asian values that the bank embraced: Respectful, Easy, and Dependable, or RED for short. This set of values was then translated into operational principles to enhance the experiences of their customers. This is done in tandem with how DBS reimagined the customer journey (as mentioned in the previous paragraph) and aligned internal processes to serve this journey. It was not just a front-end app but a constructed effort along the entire journey to help the customer navigate easily. For example, analyzing the data from their ATMS, DBS discovered that its customers spent a total of 15,000 hours a month at ATMs viewing account balances. To make it more convenient for customers, the bank launched an SMS-based banking service in 2014 from which they could carry out basic transactions, such as check balances, pay card bills, and transfer funds to their own accounts, without having to physically be at an ATM. This was the springboard for them to introduce alternative touchpoints like self-service kiosks and digital partners — convenience stores, pharmacies, supermarkets — so customers could do their banking while they were out going about their lives (Sia *et al.*, 2016). Gupta summed this up aptly:

> *There is a paradigm shift from transaction to information that has catalysed a new way of thinking about banking. As the focus for connectivity with customers shifts from the physical space to the digital and mobile spaces, banks need to develop a new engagement framework. That engagement is no longer just about products and services, but relationships and insights, and how we can leverage innovation to deliver added value to our customers.* (The Business Times, 2013)

Of course, what this also meant was that the bank had to be available to all its customers every single minute of the day. It was only logical that DBS adopt cloud technology, with which it would be able to "make the leap forward in terms of mobility, efficiency and productivity." It allowed them to reduce their reliance on physical space as well as enjoy a savings in cost: "up to 7.1x ... on hardware, 7.8x on software, and 5.8x on labour." Business processes were redesigned to include the cloud component, and DBS was able to meet its customers' demands even more quickly (IMDA, 2018).

8.2.4 *Building on a Simple Vision and Scaling Up*

DBS did not begin with any lofty ideas but an eagerness to improve their efficiency in serving their ever-growing customer base. The bank perfected this and progressed to offer more complex services. The key was to delight the customers first and then offer a wider array of services. The technology platforms they used were typically top-of-the-range systems provided by external vendors. This worked well at the start but over time, DBS became cognizant of the fact that they needed to build their own in-house capability in technology integration and that, in the longer term, would be "critical for devising sound business solutions and for staying responsive to business demands" (Sia *et al.*, 2016). In addition, DBS recognized the need to improve the bank's key processes. For each new project, "process transformation with stretch targets and measurement of outcomes" were expected. These initiatives to streamline processes proved fruitful to the tune of a S$60-million savings in the first year (Sia *et al.*, 2016).

To spearhead this process transformation, Gupta hired a new head, Paul Cobban, who proceeded to redesign all of DBS' processes, from end-to-end. Cross-functional teams were put together to reimagine a digital journey and use agile development to move toward it. Starting with a minimum viable product, DBS teams would refine, iterate, and re-release it in the field in rapid agile cycles, each time learning from customer feedback and bringing the journey closer to the reimagined version. Whenever feasible, DBS would deploy smart processing technologies as a step to building its digital IT platform. Machine learning would use experience to improve intelligent decision-making while robotic automation would take over tedious tasks. This made operations cheaper as machines performed faster and more flawlessly than human employees 24/7. They could also be integrated on top of the existing systems more quickly.

Ideally, the original plan was to build "a consistent technology platform across countries." However, this was not possible because in reality, Asian markets were diverse — they were multicultural as well as multilingual — and each one was at a different stage of development.

> *Hence, the technology platform had to be not just scalable but also flexible. Various configurable options were necessary to meet specific country requirements. Investments were made to acquire configurable enterprise systems, to reverse-engineer and modernise the legacy systems, and to adopt service-oriented architecture and enterprise application integration technologies. (Sia et al., 2016)*

8.2.5 *Collaborating and Innovating for Success*

Besides being customer-centric, DBS collaborated and innovated continuously across the entire organization. It also understood the need to look outside for opportunities to collaborate and partner when it could no longer build everything in-house.

Within the organization, DBS encouraged all its staff to be innovative, going so far as to initiate innovation training workshops for employees as well as recruiting people with a high potential to innovate (Sia *et al.*, 2016). Successful innovations were applauded and circulated to boost employee confidence as well as motivate others to step up. The bank also crowdsourced for ideas from staff, which led to the creation of uGOiGO^{TM}.

> *uGOiGO^{TM} was an online time deposit group-buy campaign started by a group of employees at DBS Hong Kong in 2013. The campaign targeted affluent customers using social media. More attractive tiered interest rates for time deposits were triggered once the deposit amounts hit specific targets. The new product launch was a tremendous success. The uGOiGO microsite generated over 64,000 page views, and acquisition of new customers by DBS Treasures (the bank's wealth management arm) grew 147 times more compared to the traditional means of customer acquisition. Total new deposits exceeded the original goal by 80%, with many of the customers being new to DBS. The viral effect of the group-buy campaign was so effective that the idea was quickly trademarked and replicated across the region. In Singapore, the campaign met its 100% target in just five days. (Sia et al., 2016)*

Internally, DBS also cast its net wide, seeking out innovations at the strategic level, particularly in "areas with high-disruptive potential for systematic incubation" (Sia *et al.*, 2016). Digital innovations could be implemented in numerous areas such as mobile banking and digital payment. In countries with a DBS presence where smartphone usage was high, such as Singapore and Hong Kong, the bank was able to use that to its advantage and test out a suite of apps that it had developed. "These apps provided customers with more features for share trading, insurance purchase, home search, virtual credit card payment and mobile point-of-sale" (Sia *et al.*, 2016).

Looking for solutions internally was only one part of the equation. DBS also sought external partnerships to help them develop its innovation ecosystem. It worked with established research institutions such as universities and partnered with technology companies (e.g., SAS, IBM) to leverage their expertise and know-how in order to gain a head start on its digital innovation.

> *For example, DBS exploited big data through IBM's Watson cognitive computing technology, which was deployed in its Wealth Management Division and subsequently rolled out to other business lines. The Watson Engagement Advisor solution used artificial intelligence to glean insights on market research and transactional behaviours in guiding relationship managers to offer advice tailored*

to a client's risk appetite and desirable investment portfolio. (Sia
et al., 2016)

The bank also collaborated with the Institute for Infocomm
Research at A*STAR (Agency for Science, Technology, and
Research) to "further develop the bank's analytics capabilities" and
"deepen its understanding of customer "footprints" and thus provide
more personalized interactions" (Sia *et al.*, 2016). That was not
all. Using accelerator programs such as Startupbootcamp FinTech,
DBS proactively reached out and connected with the tech startup
community to gain more innovative tech ideas that it could transform
into benefits for its customers (Sia *et al.*, 2016).

In all this quest for innovation, there was an element of risk;
something startups were extremely familiar with and which banks
were traditionally averse to. So why was DBS venturing into the
unknown? It saw this as "a way of getting itself ready for the future"
(Sia *et al.*, 2018) and therefore was willing to innovate and experiment
like a startup or an e-commerce company. After all, even if it failed,
the bank calculated that there would be very little impact, if any at
all. In the long run, it hoped to emulate Spanish bank, BBVA, and
become a "banking industry platform player," meaning that it would
"provide the architectural platform for banking apps" (Sia *et al.*,
2016) which other businesses can use as a base. And it looks like DBS
is on its way. As of 2020, the bank has more than 200 different readily
available application programming interfaces or APIs that can be
used to support businesses and their customer needs, and among its
partners are McDonald's, MSIG, Grab, and PropertyGuru.com.

8.2.6   *Using Omnichannels to Maximize Customer Value*

There is a need to enhance customer value by building an effective
offline-to-online banking platform that seamlessly integrates into the
customer's normal usage. Physical branches still matter for all age
groups, which means there was a need to reinvent certain branch
benefits with an improved experience.

DBS' new branch model was redesigned to showcase an
"intuitive integration of digital technologies for a new customer

experience" (Sia *et al.*, 2016). Of course, digital services would feature prominently at the branches, such as virtual queuing, tablets at the waiting area, electronic forms, and in some outlets, "separate Quick Serve Counter for non-cash transactions that could be completed within 15 minutes" (Sia *et al.*, 2016). There are also custom-made workstations, named Consultation Pods, where staff can give customers' their full attention. This reflects the bank's commitment to its Asian heritage where a human touch is still present in face-to-face engagements. In a similar manner, DBS ensured that customers who come to their branches are met by a person. This speaks of the Respectful aspect of their RED mantra "[b]ecause from an Asian service perspective, ... it's respectful to have somebody greet you" (Fitzgerald, 2014). This is what the bank terms as a "signature customer experience" (Fitzgerald, 2014).

In early 2015, DBS pioneered the SMS "Q" service, the first bank in Singapore to do so. This allowed customers to request a queue number, through an SMS, before visiting a branch. The reply message would contain information about the number of people in the various queues (personal, business, account opening, ATM card, etc.) and customers could confirm if they still wanted a number or visit the bank at another time. This also translated to more free time for some customers such that they were more open to speaking with staff about other issues, and ultimately resulted in double-digit sales growth for investment products as well as bancassurance, an arrangement in which a bank and an insurance company form a partnership so that the insurance company could sell it products to the bank's client base (Sia *et al.*, 2016).

8.3   Key Lessons Learned

8.3.1   *It Takes a Big Commitment to Transform into a Digital*

DBS epitomized the DT journey of a traditional bank. Digitalizing the bank was a priority since 2009. with CEO Piyush Gupta providing a clearly articulated strategy. Beyond funding, talent development, and agile ways of working, the organizational culture must also allow for an appetite to take some risk. According to

DBS' Chief Finance Officer, Chng Sok Hui, the digital segment had a cost-to-income ratio of about 34%, which is "20 percentage points lower compared to the traditional segment of 54 percent" (Sengupta, 2020). It was not easy attempting to infuse a digital mindset during the transition period and much depended on the leadership that was committed to radically changing the bank's direction. It meant upending HR processes to find and train the right talent, rebuilding IT systems to ensure they were sufficient modular, and having flexibility to accommodate new products and services, as well as embedding advanced analytics in processes across the entire organization to accelerate, automate, and improve decisions. It also meant that new processes and performance management systems had to be created to support a culture that learned and adapted. It called for the deployment of the best people and resources to support the transformation.

8.3.2   *Aim for Vastly Improved Performance, Not Just Productivity Improvement*

DBS took transformation began with process improvement, focusing on doing it better, faster, and cheaper. This was evidenced through the large number of PIEs initiated by the staff. The improved processes, together with available technology and better understanding of customers' banking behavior, laid the foundation for major transformation in their product portfolio. This brought the bank in line with the service expectation of customers and allowed them to compete effectively in the financial marketplace of that time.

Beyond process improvement, DBS transformation was also powered by a desire to improve customer service by leveling up their service standards. This goal provided an important framework for their transformation effort. Gradually, the bank no longer perceived it as a productivity improvement project but a transformation effort to attain a higher level of performance in every aspect of the organization.

While the bank began with process improvement to reverse the trend of falling customer satisfaction, this approach had its limitations as customer behaviors were rapidly changing. This gave rise to a need to look at their customer journey to better understand customer activities, needs, perception, and emotions. This resulted in the bank stepping out of the traditional process paradigm and moving toward a Human-Centered Design (HCD). This holistic approach allowed the bank to envision and design better banking solutions, much to the delight of their customers. In 2013, competition in financial services had intensified due to the rapid assimilation of digital technologies into all aspects of people's lives. Furthermore, digitalization had lowered the barrier of entry for FinTech startups. This new momentum forced DBS to re-examine its strategy yet again. At the same time, however, this provided the bank with an opportunity to create new business models, enter new markets, and establish new revenue streams. Seeing that digital technology had given FinTech companies a leg up in the industry, the bank decided to take a more aggressive approach to its own DT. In early 2014, DBS announced an investment of another S$200 million in digital banking initiatives over the following three years.

The leaders were convinced that DT was the way forward and were willing to bet the company's growth strategy on this. They aspired to institute a change that would propel the bank into the future. Top management was innately aware that they had the ability to pull it off, but not without the cooperation and commitment of every single person on the team. They understood that, to sustain the momentum, it was important to help employees throughout the bank to think and work toward the same goal. They ensured that the vision was not just their own but shared by every employee. Everyone was on the same page. Staff at all levels were encouraged to share whatever ideas they had to improve the way the bank handled matters, keeping customer first and foremost in their minds.

8.3.3 *A Sustainable Digital Journey Begins with Understanding, Thinking, and Planning*

DBS realized, at the start, that there was a need for thoughtful deliberation and adaptive execution. It was crucial to ensure that certain things were done right, especially understanding where the business value laid in the organization. Data analytics provided the understanding on how every process across the entire organization could be digitalized or improved. It was also important for the bank to look outside its business to understand trends, examine unmet customer needs, and identify inefficiencies in the marketplace. It was this understanding and thinking that led DBS to the options on hand, prompting it to clarify the problems that needed to be solved and figure out a way to solve it. Given the complexity of DT, DBS took some effort and time to determine the right operating model. But being slow and steady helped to ensure that implemented changes were done right and could last. They understood that quick execution without understanding and planning was definitely not the way to move forward as there were myriad organizational issues that needed to be addressed as they started to work in agile teams, organized themselves around discrete processes, products, and customer segments. There was a need to figure out where people sat, whom they reported to, what talent and systems they needed. It was also important to anticipate and spend time to map out the capabilities and people to develop so that they could help to execute the transformation.

Deliberate thinking was done so that teams could kick into a cycle of rapid development, experimentation, and iteration across a range of initiatives. Small teams, working intensively together, cutting across organizational boundaries would release minimally viable products and see how they performed before. This would allow them to adapt the product and progressively achieve cycles of continuous improvement.

8.3.4   *Important to Have Talent at All Levels*

Finding the right talent was important as it was a significant accelerator of change. There was a premium on people who were able to adapt and learn quickly, as top technical and digital practitioners were known to be up to 10 times more productive than their average peers. From an organizational perspective, the best tends to attract the best, creating a pull for top talent. With a strong brand and compelling employee value proposition, DBS was able to build a pipeline of talent to complement its DT initiatives. Concurrently, effort was made to reskill thousands of employees in the bank's existing workforce. This was done with a mix of classroom training and on-the-job learning, supported by technology.

8.4   Conclusion

DBS' DT journey really began with their digitalization effort; the main focus of this phase was to improve efficiency by apply technology to individual processes. DT took place when DBS was able to combine the disparate digital systems and processes to give its customers individualized and omnichannel experiences.

The bank's commitment to transform began with its CEO together with a few other leaders. They orchestrated and permeated their vision across the entire organization. The leaders got into the details and involved everyone in the transformation. Each transformation effort was framed to improve performance and not just to improve productivity. Driven by a common objective, it effectively inspired and drove the team involved in the transformation to achieve beyond their imagination.

The bank has developed a set of digital-enabled capabilities by putting their strategy into motion. Customer journey mapping, coupled with a new business model design, enabled them to offer customer-centric services so as to better engage their customers.

To sustain the transformation effort, DBS invested substantially in its people and culture, and its leaders made tremendous efforts to engage and continuously remind all stakeholders to ensure they appreciate why the bank needed to transform. To weather through future challenges, particular attention was paid to sustain newly acquired execution discipline.

At present, DBS is able to fundamentally reimagine the way it operates and engages its customers and other stakeholders. It has reconceived banking from a customer perspective, and that has entailed redesigning the bank's services within and with its ecosystem partners to most effectively deliver compelling and unique customer experiences.

References

The Business Times (2013). Banking's Technology Challenge, May 29, pp. 28, 30.

A. R. Choudhury (2015). Using IT to be Nimble and Innovative. *The Business Times*, March 16. Retrieved from https://www.businesstimes.com.sg/foc us/in-depth/cio-speaks/using-it-to-be-nimble-and-innovative (Accessed 20 November 2020).

M. C. Christensen, K. Dillon, T. Hall, and D. S. Duncan (2016). *Competing Against Luck: The Story of Innovation and Customer Choice* (Harper Business, New York, NY).

DBS (2010). Letter to Shareholders. DBS Annual Report 2010. Retrieved from https://www.dbs.com/annualreports/2010/letter_to_shareholders.htm #2 (Accessed 20 November 2020).

DBS (2016). DBS Launches India's First Mobile-only Bank, Heralds 'WhatsApp Moment in Banking,' April 26. Retrieved from https://www.dbs.com/ newsroom/DBS_launches_Indias_first_mobile_only_bank_heralds_WhatsApp_ moment_in_banking (Accessed 20 November 2020).

DBS (2018a). DBS Signals Time Has Come For New Kind of Banking, May 15. Retrieved from https://www.dbs.com/newsroom/DBS_signals_time_has_com e_for_new_kind_of_banking (Accessed 20 November 2020).

DBS (2018b). DBS named Global Bank of the Year by leading Financial Times publication, *The Banker*, November 30. Retrieved from https://www.dbs.co m/newsroom/DBS_named_Global_Bank_of_the_Year (Accessed 20 November 2020).

DBS (2019a). DBS Bank to Expand in India With Establishment of Wholly-Owned Subsidiary, March 4. Retrieved from https://www.dbs. com/newsroom/DBS_bank_to_expand_in_India_with_establishment_of_wholly_ owned_subsidiary (Accessed 20 November 2020).

DBS (2019b). DBS Breaks New Ground With Global Hackathon, May 28. Retrieved from https://www.dbs.com/newsroom/DBS_breaks_new_ground_ with_global_hackathon (Accessed 20 November 2020).

DBS (2020). DBS named Asia's Safest Bank for 12th consecutive year. Retrieved from https://www.dbs.com/newsroom/DBS_named_Asias_Safest_Bank_for_ 12th_consecutive_year (Accessed 20 November 2020).

M. Fitzgerald (2014). DBS Bank Pumps Up the Volume on its Technology. *MIT Sloan Management Review*, January 6. Retrieved from https://sloanreview .mit.edu/article/dbs-bank-pumps-up-the-volume-on-its-technology/ (Accessed 20 November 2020).

J. Grant (2018). Transforming a Traditional Bank into an Agile Market Leader. *Strategy+Business*, December 19. Retrieved from https://www.str ategy-business.com/article/Transforming-a-Traditional-Bank-into-an-Agile-Market-Leader?gko=036bf (Accessed 20 November 2020).

R. Hartung (2017). How Digitisation Powers DBS to Profitability. *The Asian Banker*, August 10. Retrieved from http://www.theasianbanker.com/upd ates-and-article/how-digitisation-powers-dbs-to-profitability (Accessed 20 November 2020).

IMDA (2018). The Future of Services: Services and Digital Economy Technology Roadmap. Infocomm Media Development Authority. Retrieved from https://www.imda.gov.sg/-/media/Imda/Files/Industry-Development/Infrastructure/Technology/Technology-Roadmap/SDE-TRM-Main-Report.pdf (Accessed 20 November 2020).

W. Lim (2017). How DBS Transformed Into a Digital Powerhouse. Cooler Insights, May 3. Retrieved from https://coolerinsights.com/2017/05/dbs-digital-business/ (Accessed 20 November 2020).

MAS (2019). MAS to Issue Up to Five Digital Bank Licences, June 28. Retrieved from https://www.mas.gov.sg/news/media-releases/2019/mas-to-issue-up-to-five-digital-bank-licences (Accessed 20 November 2020).

A. Mccord and M. D. Boone (2008). Technologies and Services in Support of Virtual Workplaces. In P. Zemliansky and K. St. Amant (Eds.), *Handbook of Research on Virtual Workplaces and the New Nature of Business Practices* (Information Science Reference, New York, NY), pp. 346–363.

D. Paperny (2015). An Interview with Neal Cross. *FST Media*, February 18. Retrieved from https://fst.local2.weebpal.com/features/interview-neal-cross (Accessed 20 November 2020).

PwC (2019). Digital Banks Get Real in Singapore. PwC Singapore, August. Retrieved from https://www.pwc.com/sg/en/publications/digital-banks-get-real-in-singapore.html (Accessed 20 November 2020).

M. Rosen, T. Krichevsky and H. Sharma (2000). Strategies for a Sustainable Enterprise. In B. Unhelkar (Ed.), *Handbook of Research on Green ICT: Technology, Business and Social Perspectives (2 volumes)* (Information Science Reference, New York, NY), pp. 1–28.

J. Sengupta (2020). Becoming More Than a Bank: Digital Transformation at DBS. McKinsey & Company Financial Services, January 9. Retrieved from https://www.mckinsey.com/industries/financial-services/our-insights/banking-matters/becoming-more-than-a-bank-digital-transformation-at-dbs (Accessed 20 November 2020).

K. S. Sia, C. Soh and P. Weill (2016). How DBS Bank Pursued a Digital Business Strategy. *MIS Quarterly Executive*, **15**(2), 105–121.

R. Speculand [@speculand] (2020). "If You Want to Compete You Must Embrace Technology. Which Means Not Just Technology Change But a Culture Change," [Tweet]. Twitter. Retrieved from https://twitter.com/speculand/status/1256051969661304832 (Accessed 20 November 2020).

J. Tan (2014). Piyush Gupta Demands a Shift to Digital Banking in Singapore. *Forbes*, June 4. Retrieved from https://www.forbes.com/sites/forbesasia/2014/06/04/piyush-gupta-wants-a-shift-to-digital-banking-in-singapore/#66eebac65452 (Accessed 20 November 2020).

Y. Yahya (2016). Live More, Bank Less: DBS Takes the Chore Out of Banking. *The Straits Times*, March 14. Retrieved from https://www.straitstimes.com/business/banking/live-more-bank-less-dbs-takes-the-chore-out-of-banking (Accessed 20 November 2020).

Index

Singapore University of Social Sciences - World Scientific Future Economy Series

www.ingramcontent.com/pod-product-compliance
Lightning Source LLC
Chambersburg PA
CBHW061253220326
41599CB00028B/5628